Reflection in Action

Additional titles in the **Actionable Research for Social Justice in Education and Society series:**

Research, Actionable Knowledge, and Social Change
Reclaiming Social Responsibility Through Research Partnerships
Edward P. St. John

Intersectionality and Research in Education
A Guidebook for Higher Education and Student Affairs Professionals
Dannielle Joy Davis, Rachelle Brunn, and James Olive
Publication date: Summer 2014

Using Action Inquiry in Education Reform
A Guide
Edward P. St. John, Kim Lijana, and Glenda Musoba
Publication date: September 2015

Critical Action Research
A Guide for Students and Practitioners
Leticia Bustillos and Edlyn Peña
Publication date: September 2015

Series Coeditors:
Edward P. St. John, University of Michigan
Penny A. Pasque, University of Oklahoma
Shaun R. Harper, The University of Pennsylvania
Estela Bensimon, University of Southern California

Reflection in Action

A Guidebook for Student Affairs Professionals and Teaching Faculty

Edited by Kimberly A. Kline

Foreword by Edward P. St. John

STERLING, VIRGINIA

COPYRIGHT © 2014 BY
STYLUS PUBLISHING, LLC.

Published by Stylus Publishing, LLC
22883 Quicksilver Drive
Sterling, Virginia 20166-2102

**Library of Congress Cataloging-in-Publication Data for this title
has been applied for.**

13-digit ISBN: 978-1-57922-828-6 (cloth)
13-digit ISBN: 978-1-57922-829-3 (paper)
13-digit ISBN: 978-1-57922-830-9 (library networkable e-edition)
13-digit ISBN: 978-1-57922-831-6 (consumer e-edition)

Printed in the United States of America

All first editions printed on acid-free paper
that meets the American National Standards Institute
Z39-48 Standard.

Bulk Purchases

Quantity discounts are available for use in workshops and for
staff development.
Call 1-800-232-0223

First Edition, 2014

10   9   8   7   6   5   4   3   2   1

To my father, Chas; and grandmother, Annie, who both empowered me to grow brave by reflection

CONTENTS

and Social Agency

7. Reflection in Action
    Exploring Race and Culture in Critical Reflective Pedagogy   *103*
      Pamela Petrease Felder

8. Teaching Professional Development in Higher Education
    and Student Affairs   *121*
    Unless
      Stacy A. Jacob

9. Moving From Social Justice to Social Agency   *133*
    Keeping It Messy
      Penny A. Pasque and Brittany Harris

PART FOUR   Moving Forward

10. Implications for Daily Practice and Life   *155*
      Kimberly A. Kline

    Chapter Reflection Questions   *167*

    About the Editor and Contributors   *173*

    Index   *177*

FOREWORD

*R*eflection in Action: A Guidebook for Student Affairs Professionals and Teaching Faculty is the second book in the new Stylus series, Actionable Research for Social Justice in Education and Society. This series was created to fill a void in the literature on colleges and their students: the gap between theory and practice in leadership, administration, and teaching. We encourage scholarship that advances theory and practice through actionable research addressing critical challenges that emerge within professional practice.

The gap in the field results, at least in part, from the didactic nature of the literature: Most theory and research either focuses on the functional mechanisms used by governments, institutions, and both academic and student affairs units within colleges and universities *or* provides critiques of these frameworks. There are robust literatures on practice of administration, teaching, and student affairs in higher education that fall into these functional categories, along with extensive critiques that identify crises and advocate solutions—new practices that will remedy persistent problems. But defining problems that emerge in practice as crises that require set types of solutions constrains action and often perpetuates inequality. After decades of this dialectic between functional approaches and critiques of them, we must recognize that this discursive process has perpetuated a stratified system that reinforces social inequality.

An alternative is to engage in actionable inquiries that inform efforts to promote social justice within educational systems. This not only includes encouraging action research by practitioners and faculty, but also new forms of research partnerships that encourage and inform strategies for systemic change, along with development and refinement of methods and methodologies that promote and inform reform, the aims of this new book series.

Kim Kline's edited volume focuses on a topic at the core of actionable knowledge: reflection in action. The authors in this volume address a range of topics related to student affairs administration and teaching of future leaders in this field with a focus on reflective processes. Change that integrates social justice into practice involves building an understanding of current practice, envisioning workable alternatives, testing these alternative forms of practice in action settings, and adapting strategies based on insights gained through this process. Reflecting in action is part of each step of the process.

Our ability to reflect critically on our own actions within practice provides insights into the reasons why the system works and doesn't work, alternative ways of conceiving of practice, and learning as we adapt practice.

Teaching of reflection in action is closely linked to practice, but also involves reflecting on information—trends in outcomes and relation research. At the most basic level, this involves observing and relating what actually happens to what we thought would happen when we acted. Of course, research on outcomes is an important source of information—and we need to use trend data and research as we review the links between practice and outcomes—but practitioners, teachers, and researchers also need to reflect and adapt. This requires moving beyond self-sealing assumptions that we already know the best solutions.

This book will be useful to higher education practitioners, teaching professionals, and those working in student affairs, who seek to discover new solutions to social inequality through reflection and adaptation that builds artistry of practice. Instructors will also benefit from the reflection in action framework as it applies to their own teaching and learning practices. Lastly, it is appropriate for higher education and student affairs master's and doctoral programs that focus on administration and leadership.

Edward P. St. John
University of Michigan, Ann Arbor

ACKNOWLEDGMENTS

Ed St. John has been an incredible mentor. From the early days of our interactions, we exchanged colorful debates about whether or not master's students were ready to engage in conversations regarding the intersection of social justice issues and professional development. Instead of rebutting my view, he encouraged me to seek out the answer to this question through a myriad of approaches and opportunities. I was able to experiment first as a student in his Professional Development course, next as a teaching assistant in that same course, and then as a coinstructor and action researcher within his classroom. Ed's approach was participatory, allowed me to learn through discovery, and served as the quintessential form of role modeling reflection in action. His challenge and support have given me the confidence to be a caring faculty member and I now continue this work through the Professional Development and Communities of Practice course, whereby I can pay forward his generous spirit.

The importance of having colleagues (Megan Moore Gardner, Marilee Bresciani, Eric Jackson, Richanne Mankey, Wanda Davis, Amy Wilson, Kim Harvey) and students (Greg Newman, Shakira Henderson, Lavere Foster, Rhina Duquela) with whom I can have frank conversations and can test my assumptions has proven to be invaluable.

A special thank you to my two favorite editors: my mom, Bernice Kline Pudup; and Phyllis Craiger Stillman. And finally, to Don, my spiritual advisor; and Dima, my biggest cheerleader.

INTRODUCTION

The student affairs profession has concentrated its focus on studying the learning and development of the college-going public. As a result, the majority of time spent in graduate classrooms is spent studying students. Somewhere along the way, we have lost sight of the care and nurturing of ourselves as student affairs professionals that is imperative if we are to survive a full career in our chosen profession. Recently, I attended a keynote presentation by Eric Stoller, a rising star who blogs about social media within the student affairs profession. He posed this question: "Do you realize that while all of you are chained to your computers answering work e-mails, there is an entire culture-in-conversation happening without you?" What Stoller was suggesting is that Twitter will soon surpass e-mail as a primary mode of communication among individuals on college campuses. This concept was liberating to me, because I go through a daily reconciliation between the time I spend answering e-mail and the time I spend with my students. This revelation caused me to realize the urgency of the conversation that we've created in this book.

Reflection in Action provides a road map that has been missing in graduate study by illustrating a new approach to dealing with dialogues that are difficult in particular for the paraprofessional or new professional to navigate. Graduate programs provide a wealth of opportunities for students to study psychosocial developmental theories. Some graduate programs have even evolved to a point where multiculturalism is woven into courses throughout the curriculum. What is missing, however, is a deliberate infusion of activities and examples that can be practiced within safe spaces. The ethic of care, which we encourage in our undergraduates, is absent from the development of the professional in student affairs. With rapidly changing demographics and modes of communication, it is more important than ever to deconstruct professional dialogue through a social justice lens. There are several articles that address different forms of multiculturalism, and there are a number of publications available for faculty, staff, and graduate students in the area of multicultural competence, such as *Multicultural Competence in Student Affairs* (Pope, Reynolds, & Mueller, 2004) and multicultural awareness, and scores on multicultural knowledge (e.g., King & Howard-Hamilton, 2003) and multiple identities (e.g., Gayles & Kelly, 2007). The topics of privilege (e.g., Castellanos, Gloria, Mayorga, & Salas 2007; Lechuga, Clerc, & Howell, 2009) and models of oppression (e.g., Edwards, 2006; Freire, 2002; Kivel, 2002) are the focus of many scholarly articles. Although these publications are noteworthy, they overlook the professional development of higher education and student affairs practitioners-in-training. Students learn about theories, identities, ways of knowing, and research on college students and administration, but do not have ample opportunities to reflect upon and integrate those theories into practice (Nottingham, 1998). In many cases, social justice issues are treated at an espoused level, but insufficient attention is given to the practice of social justice and social agency education in student affairs administration. To understand and resolve this dilemma, it is important to focus on research that creates paths toward actionable change within higher education and student affairs master's and doctoral programs.

Reflection in Action uses St. John (2009) as a stepping-off point to discuss the growing gap between "the techniques and reasoning advocated by and conveyed in professional education and the moral reasoning used in practice" (p. xi). In higher education and student affairs master's programs, it is necessary for professors to rethink their curriculum to infuse methods that help students practice such techniques and reasoning in order to narrow the gap. The purpose of this guidebook is to invigorate student affairs professionals and higher education faculty alike to create new approaches when discussing sensitive/controversial topics with their students. The intent of this text is to provide professionals with a critical social understanding of current social justice, social agency, reflection, and actionable knowledge in order to offer new and successful pathways for practice. We encourage you to think about the role you play in educating our new professionals to become wise, ethical, caring citizens of the college community in the same way that we help undergraduate students become wise citizens of their greater community.

In a collection of 10 chapters, exceptional teachers, scholars, and professionals provide a diverse and alternative lens through which to examine the intersection of social justice, education, and professional practice in our field. The text is organized by three overarching themes. Part One explores existing theories, examining claims, and proposing new understandings. In Chapter 1, "Seizing Responsibility: Using Actionable Knowledge to Promote Fairness," Edward P. St. John discusses the importance of social responsibility and moral consciousness in higher education and student affairs professional practice. Megan Moore Gardner, in Chapter 2, "Actionable Knowledge and Student Affairs," introduces the concept of action research as a platform for professionals to ask questions and conduct research in an effort to improve self and society. In Chapter 3, "Evolution of a Moral and Caring Professional,"

Kathleen M. Boyle provides an overview of the moral reasoning literature along with insights for integrating justice and care into our daily practice.

Part Two explores concrete tools and safe spaces for practicing difficult dialogues in professional practice. In Chapter 4, "Critical Social Dialogues and Reflecting in Action," Shakira Henderson and I offer guidance and strategies for practicing difficult dialogues and reflection in action in professional practice. In Chapter 5, "The Game Changers: Moving Beyond Isms to Restore Civility to the Academy," Wanda M. Davis provides a provocative look at the hierarchy of isms that different societal groups face and provides tools and environmental examples for transcending this perceived hierarchy. In Chapter 6, "Dialogue, Reflection, and Learning: From Our (Spiritual) Center," Richanne C. Mankey describes practical methods that assist us in knowing where we are, so that we can meet students where they are, in order to be successful in assisting their development.

Part Three, which explores professional development, action research, and social agency, provides a road map for professionals wishing to live their careers through reflecting in action. In Chapter 7, "Reflection in Action: Exploring Race and Culture in Critical Reflective Pedagogy," Pamela Petrease Felder presents a model using the teaching narrative as a practical response to the racial crisis in American higher education and explores how the teaching narrative can serve as a preparation strategy for the teaching of race and culture in the classroom, through faculty-student interactions and for professional development and teaching evaluation. In Chapter 8, "Teaching Professional Development in Higher Education and Student Affairs: Unless," Stacy A. Jacob discusses the dilemma of the disconnect between the learning of theory and opportunities to reflect upon and integrate theory into practice. This chapter focuses on research that creates paths toward actionable change within higher education and student affairs programs. In Chapter 9, "Moving From Social Justice to Social Agency: Keeping It Messy," Penny A. Pasque and Brittany Harris discuss the transition of individuals from aligning with a group, cause, or reading for a class that is "socially just" to acting as social agents as reflected in the ethical standards for the field. And in Part Four, "Moving Forward," in Chapter 10, "Implications for Daily Practice and Life," I provide insights and applications for daily practice.

References

Castellanos, J., Gloria, A., Mayorga, M., & Salas, C. (2007). Student affairs professionals' self-report of multicultural competence: Understanding awareness, knowledge, and skills. *NASPA Journal, 44*(4), 643–663.

Edwards. T. (2006). *Cultures of masculinity*. New York: Routltedge.

Freire, P. (2002). *Education for critical consciousness.* New York: The Continuum Publishing Company.

Gayles, J., & Kelly, B. (2007). Experiences with diversity in the curriculum: Implications for graduate programs and student affairs practice. *NASPA Journal, 44,* 193–208.

King, P. M., & Howard-Hamilton, M. F. (2003). An assessment of multicultural competence. *NASPA Journal, 40*(2), 119–133.

Kivel, P. (2002). *Uprooting racism.* British Columbia, Canada: New Society Publishers.

Lechuga, V. M., Clerc, L. N., & Howell, A. K. (2009). Power, privilege, and learning: Facilitating encountered situations to promote social justice. *Journal of College Student Development, 50*(2), 229–244.

Nottingham, J. E. (1998). Using self-reflection for personal and professional development in student affairs. In W. Bryan & R. Schwartz (Eds.), *New directions for student services: Strategies for staff development: Personal and professional education in the 21st century 84,* 71–81. San Francisco, CA: Jossey-Bass.

Pope, R. L., Reynolds, A. L., & Muller, J. A. (2004). Multicultural competence in student affairs. San Francisco: Jossey-Bass.

St. John, E. P. (2009). *Action, reflection and social justice: Integrating moral reasoning into professional education.* Cresskill, NJ: Hampton Press.

PART ONE

EXISTING THEORIES, EXAMINING CLAIMS, AND PROPOSING NEW UNDERSTANDINGS

1

SEIZING RESPONSIBILITY

Using Actionable Knowledge to Promote Fairness

Edward P. St. John

A spiring student affairs professionals enter their master's and doctoral programs with prior experiences that inspired their choice of a specialized field in which to support students' navigation of education systems. Twenty-first century universities differ from those of the midtwentieth century, the period during which most theories of college student development originated. Society is more diverse, a consequence of both changing demographics and the internationalization of educational opportunities. The idea of globalization is central to higher education in the twenty-first century, and it is crucial that student affairs administrators and aspiring professionals develop skills that encourage openness to learning about the perspectives of others as they navigate their educational and career pathways and encourage others to make informed choices in an increasingly diverse society. This chapter makes two interrelated arguments: (a) Both current and aspiring professionals in student affairs share responsibility for promoting fairness and equity in educational systems; and (b) assuming this responsibility provides opportunities for developing and using actionable knowledge in the process of change and adaptation within colleges and universities in globalizing societies.

Social Responsibility in Context

We live and work in colleges and universities transitioning to universal opportunity for access, but there are growing inequalities owing to failures of school reform in many locales, resistance to affirmative action in states with elite institutions of public higher education, and inadequacies in public funding for need-based student aid. The result is a paradox: In spite of growing access, social stratification is increasing. Although college may now be a necessity for gaining or maintaining access to middle-class professions across generations (e.g., business administration, education, engineering, health care), gaining access to and staying in college is a complicated matter. Although student affairs professionals are not responsible for these conditions in their colleges and universities, recognition of the contemporary context for student life in universities is a starting point for encouraging students in their efforts to navigate educational systems and for professionals to collaborate on the design and testing of remedies to problems in the educational system.

Globalization and Academic Life

The emphasis on expanding the number of people with advanced education in science and engineering is a commonality among nations engaged in the global economy. Although workforce policies in the United States emphasize employment in high-paying technical jobs (Commission on the Skills of the American Workforce, 2007), the same arguments prevail in the international literature on access (Yang, 2011; Yang & St. John, in press). Indeed the culture of global competitiveness is now not only evident in public policy, but is also deeply embedded in the experiences of students as they develop college aspirations, choose a college, and navigate academic pathways.

Institutions also face new pressures that differ from the ones faced in the liberal arts culture that prevailed in undergraduate education in the mid-twentieth century when student development theory was originally developed. Indeed, the idea that students should use their first two years to choose a major is being replaced by new pressures to promote persistence in STEM fields (science, technology, engineering, and math), which essentially limits student choices because of the constrained curriculum required to prepare for advanced course work in these fields (St. John & Musoba, 2010). Parents and older siblings also often pressure students to choose majors that emphasize science and technology (St. John, Hu, & Fisher, 2011). There is a stress on improving diversity and promoting learning environments that support diversity (e.g., Gurin, Dey, Hurtado, & Gurin, 2002; Hurtado, Milem, Clayton-Pederson, & Allen, 1998). Thus, professionals in higher education and student affairs confront many circumstances that undermine the espoused goals related to the development of global and social consciousness as they engage in overcoming recurrent, historic patterns of conflict within educational organizations.

Social Justice as a Goal in Student Affairs In a global context that supports diversity, the student affairs profession is at the intersection of the new goals of diversity and social justice and the older traditions of liberal education with its history of elitism. The American College Personnel Association (ACPA) supports an ethical code for the profession:

> These standards are: 1) Professional Responsibility and Competence; 2) Student Learning and Development; 3) Responsibility to the Institution; and 4) Responsibility to Society. . . . Student affairs professionals should strive to develop the virtues, or habits of behavior, that are characteristic of people in helping professions. Contextual issues must also be taken into account. Such issues include, but are not limited to, culture, temporality (issues bound by time), and phenomenology (individual perspective) and community norms. Because of the complexity of ethical conversation and dialogue, the skill of simultaneously confronting differences in perspective and respecting the rights of persons to hold different perspectives becomes essential. (ACPA, 2006, pp. 1–2)

This statement conveys the duality of the profession. On the one hand, the profession itself is situated within the concepts of professional responsibility, including responsibility to the institution and society. Yet the statement concludes that "simultaneously confronting differences in perspectives and respecting the rights of persons to hold different perspectives becomes essential." This places the concepts of justice and fairness as central to the profession.

Universities as Global and Local Contexts   Institutions of higher education are typically far from being socially just environments, and student affairs professionals frequently find themselves in a position of having to represent the voices of students marginalized by the system. Some of the forces that marginalize students who are historically underrepresented include:

- *Institutionalism*: Historically established patterns of behavior reinforced by bureaucratic behavior and therefore resistant to change
- *Managerialism*: The use of decentralized authority structures, supported by modern management methods (i.e., data systems and formal and informal rules of the system)
- *Corporatization*: Systems of reporting and accountability that reinforce rigidities in systems and recurrent patterns of inequality
- *Marketization*: Shifts in the funding of higher education, including student aid (e.g., use of loans rather than need-based grants), that increase the challenges of those least able to pay the costs of continued enrollment in the educational system

These systemic forces frequently come into direct conflict with the aims of the profession, especially the idea of simultaneously confronting diverse perspectives and representing the rights of people. The practice of this ideal can be especially difficult for new professionals in the field, particularly when their organizational superiors have tacitly accepted the institutional norms and practices that have created inequalities and marginalized those who are most underrepresented because of their life circumstances.

Pillars of Moral Responsibility As new professionals engaged in their graduate education in higher education and student affairs gain experience of professionals, they are frequently confronted by challenges that test their character. In my first decades as a professor in the field, I conducted several action studies related to teaching leadership and on interventions in schools and colleges that promoted justice and fairness. I engaged in "action experiments" that involved working with students to test theories of action in practice (St. John, 2009a). Through this process, I reached five critical understandings about professional development:

1. The individual professional is responsible for moral centering and action. Faculty and interventionists should not advocate values, but rather facilitate discourse on difficult and problematic issues in practice.
2. Moral development in adulthood involves centering one's self in the ethics of both justice and care. Professionals of all types bear responsibility for their own moral development as professionals—a lifelong task.
3. There are gaps between the espoused theories of practice held by most professionals and their actions as practitioners. Learning how to engage in practices that reduce these gaps is crucial to professional development and moral consciousness.
4. Human development through adulthood creates opportunities for professional growth and potential for conscious action, especially if the inherent sequence of learning about self and practice is realized and acted upon.
5. Post-conventional moral reasoning involves critical and spiritual reflection on morally problematic situations along with testing strategies that might transform them. (From St. John, 2009a, pp. 17–22)

We can view these understandings within the developmental process in student affairs:

1. As undergraduates, students learn about the student affairs profession and develop inner commitments that lead them to the field of study (restated understanding 1).

2. Study of the field of higher education and student affairs provides means of centering oneself in the codified content along with moral and ethical codes of the field (restated understanding 2).
3. When new professionals enter practice they are confronted by the gaps between espoused intent, as defined by the values of the field, and actual behaviors in colleges and universities, reinforced by the formal system (restated understanding 3).
4. As students grow and develop as professionals in the field, they have many opportunities to learn about themselves, their institutions, and the role of student affairs in promoting care and justice (restated understanding 4).
5. If these practices are centered within one's own core values, there are opportunities for self-actualization and integration (restated understanding 5).

Making our way through this journey of professional life requires building a personal process of *professional learning*, uncovering gaps between values and action, coupled with the process of experimenting with alternative approaches to remedying challenges that emerge.

Social Agency in Action

My argument is that professional learning provides us means of dealing with issues of social injustice and inequality within professional practice, a process of *seizing responsibility as a professional*, an ideal that is entirely consistent with the ethical code of professional development in higher education and student affairs, as stated in the ACPA ethical code. This argument was fundamentally influenced by listening to concerns raised by students in courses I taught, including Kim Kline when she was enrolled in my graduate course on professional development at Indiana University. I review the ways Kim's interventions and questioning challenged me to rethink the role of social agency in professional practice before noting the importance of theory reconstruction as an inner guiding force in professional development.

Kline Contests Functionalist Reasoning I had used a case method of teaching (Arygris, Putnam, & Smith, 1985; Argyris & Schön, 1974) for more than a decade before Kim showed up in my class. Kim not only had her master's in student affairs when she started the doctoral program at IU, but she had prior professional experience; she was an experienced professional returning for a doctoral degree.

Kim's case for the class, which is included with her permission in *College Organization and Professional Development* (St. John, 2009b), provides an example of an adaptive, strategic intervention that did not test assumptions, but did promote fairness. Specifically when working as an advisory to a student leadership group, she listened as the president of the student organization dismissed a request by a minority group to have a booth at a student event. When the case arose, the student president dismissed it with comments that seemed racist at the time. Kim did not ask questions in the public situation about the reasoning for dismissing the request, because she feared increasing the racial unrest. Instead, asserting her authority, she intervened in a way that enabled the minority student group to participate in the event as they had intended. This intervention promoted the social agency of a group that had been subject to discrimination, but did not surface and address the underlying problem in the public situation.

This case raised an issue that had concerned me for decades, since I was a graduate student. Her case used a strategic intervention to turn the course of a conversation with student leaders from a racist solution to one that was more inclusive. Yet when we used the theory of Argyris and Schön (1974) to analyze the case, it was classified as Model I, because it was closed to public testing of the core idea in the intervention, even though it changed the course of action. I had always been troubled that the original theory was situated in the functionalist theory of organizations and could only be implemented in top-down organization, that is, when leaders in the organization realized the need for—and actualized the practice of—open discourses about commitment to theories of action and intervention methods.

My insight from our class discussion of Kim's case was what was needed to distinguish the social agency of student affairs professionals from the institutional roles they played, to better understand the conflict between those two roles. I subsequently worked with Kim on an action experiment that further tested the idea of social justice as a central factor in professional development (Kline, 2007). Not only did I encourage Kline along her path, I began to more seriously ponder the problem of professional development and lack of sound theories of action to inform adult development pathways traveled by people who developed and used actionable knowledge to make changes in pursuit of social justice, a central goal of student affairs professionals in higher education.

Reconstructing Theories of Action This brings us to another, closely related core issue: the need for a theory of the development of moral reasoning compatible with the professional pathways people can potentially travel as they attempt to reconcile and reduce gaps between their espoused values and their actual practices within their profession. This led toward the reconstruction of the concepts used by Kohlberg (1981, 1984), Habermas (1990, 2003), and

Argyris (1993). The resulting framework for thinking through professional and personal trajectories toward maturity and moral judgment, reflecting understanding—and the social agency—of others, is presented in Table 1.1.

The frames of action illuminate an underlying developmental sequence of frames of professional reasoning, and the moral dimension distinguishes

TABLE 1.1
FRAMEWORK FOR REFRAMING THE RELATIONSHIP BETWEEN MORAL REASONING AND PROFESSIONAL ACTION

Levels of Moral Reasoning/ Frames of Action	Preconventional Moral Reasoning	Conventional Moral Reasoning	Postconventional Moral Reasoning
Institutionalist/ basic frames	Use rules without considering underlying problems.	Apply rules of practice consistent with ethical codes.	Use extant methods to address moral challenges.
Closed strategic frames	Adapt methods to achieve ends without considering moral problems created by new practices.	Adapt methods to address challenges; attempt to reconcile ethics within rules of practice.	Adapt strategies to address moral challenges, including issues that challenge the rules of practice.
Open strategic frames	Collaborate on strategies that use power and persuasion to achieve aims with little regard for consequences.	Collaboratively develop goals and adapt strategies to achieve the mission; reconcile strategies with ethical standards.	Collectively consider strategies for adapting mission to address client concerns, diversity, and issues of justice.
Communicative frames	Reach a false consensus within professional groups; use beliefs to construct rationales that reinforce problems in practice; fail to consider diverse voices and dissent.	Focus on actions consistent with ethical standards; consider ambiguities between ethical codes and organizational strategies; may emphasize resolving moral ambiguities.	Openly reconstruct rules (practices and methods) to address moral challenges, including diverse views and evidence of effects of action; be willing to reconstruct theories of action to address challenges.

Source: Adapted from St. John, 2013.

among three types of reasoning: *conventional*, which involves working within the rules of the system; *preconventional*, engaging in breaking or "working around" the rules to achieve goals or solve problems; and *postconventional*, which involves addressing critical issues while also considering the limitations of the rules. The four types of framing are:

- The institutionalist frame, which situates professional action and problem solving within the institutional rules system using expertise;
- The closed strategic frame, which involves aiding schools in adaptations through the use of professional discretion to solve problems;
- The open strategic frame, which involves enabling conversation within organizations to address problems confronted as groups work on the initiatives of the organization; and
- The communicative frame, which focuses on solving social critical problems that emerge within systems as a central form of action.

There is an underlying sequence of skill development within these frameworks. For example, a person needs to understand the institutional rules in relation to professional knowledge (institutionalist frame) before adapting professional practices in problem solving (closed strategic). At the same time, the actual behavior that goes on in a specific problematic situation can be analyzed using the descriptive content within these 12 categorical frames. In *College Organization and Professional Development*, I provide more detail and guidance for using the frames to analyze organizational problems (St. John, 2009b), whereas in *Research, Actionable Knowledge, and Social Change*, I discuss ways of using organizational assessment to devise ways of using action inquiry in organizational and social problem solving (St. John, 2013).

Actionable Knowledge

Actionable knowledge—the insights, imagination, evidence, and theories of action we use to navigate educational systems and encourage others to develop these skills—is crucial in student affairs administration. The increasing diversity of educational systems in the global period requires us to think about evidence from practices in ways that respect the voices of—and the experiences of—students and prospective students whose backgrounds differ from our own. I encourage use of reflective evaluation as a means of developing a learning orientation in professional practice.

Action Inquiry

The action inquiry model provides a framework for integrating research into professional practice and organizational change (St. John, 2009b, 2013).

That process involves assessing problematic situations, organizing to address the underlying challenges, and using action inquiry to address them. In this section, I focus on the ways student affairs professionals can use reflective evaluation in problem solving.

Integrating Reflective Evaluation Into Practice The idea that there are "best practices" that can be implemented to promote excellence substantially over-simplifies the complexity of organizational life in universities, especially in circumstances that involve promoting opportunities and encouraging success for individuals from historically underrepresented groups. It is essential to think about a practice, using reflective and analytic methods to determine why problems exist and how they might be solved, and to try out solutions as experiments. Viewing action as an inquiry process involves treating what we do as "pilot tests" of action strategies, recognizing that we can improve our artistry of practice. This process is integral to the concept of reflective practice in the professions (Schön, 1987). Figure 1.1 illustrates this reflective process with an explicit focus on the role of reflective evaluation—the small loop in the actionable method—as a means of integrating reflection into practice.

My recommendation for graduate students and beginning practitioners in student affairs is to begin by reflecting on critical challenges they have faced in their work as professionals. The case method illustrated in *College Organization and Professional Development* (St. John, 2009b) provides a framework and examples of how to do this. I strongly encourage professionals at all stages to integrate reflection into practice. It is necessary to take this step, which provides a foundation for using evaluative information to inform

Figure 1.1 Integrating the Evaluation Into Action Inquiry

Source: Adapted from St. John, Lijana, & Musoba, 2013.

practice, before we can turn the pressure of accountability systems into strategies for advocacy for underrepresented groups.

Closing the Loop There is a big difference between (a) viewing practice as implementation of rules and practices thought to be "best," and (b) reflecting on practice and developing one's own thoughts on what strategies are best. The process of reflection on past practices using appropriate forms of evaluative evidence ranges from reflections on experiences to quantitative analyses of outcomes of interventions. Becoming an authentic reflective practitioner begins with looking back on problematic situations in our experience and considering them as "cases" we can analyze. When we take the stance of treating normal practice as a pilot test of actionable strategies, we open the door to reflective practice.

The dominant concept of educational research emphasizes replication of practices that are statistically associated with successful outcomes. But this concept is divorced from the ongoing process of leadership and organizational practice, because it does not integrate evidence generated through research. The development of actionable knowledge requires us to think differently about both research evidence and reflection on and in practice. Reflection *on* practice can be retrospective, as we think back about and analyze professional situations we have encountered as cases, whereas reflection *in* practice involves using these reflections in challenging situations and adjusting how we handle work situations when problems emerge.

Forms of Actionable Knowledge

To move from scientific theories of practice to actionable knowledge involves: using our insights about problems to explore critical issues, imagining alternative practices to current practice, and gathering evidence about the relationships between actions and outcomes to test our assumptions (i.e., tacit theories of action). This process provides us with information we can use to navigate educational systems and to encourage others to develop these skills. I outline three straightforward and interrelated ways to generate and use evidence to inform our own navigation of systems and encourage others to build their social and educational navigational skills.

Personal Reflection on and in Action In classes using reflective practice methods, I ask students to develop a case that involves reflecting on a problematic situation using a format developed by Argyris and Schön (1974). Students typically raise troubling problems, not unlike Kim's case noted previously. When I was finally able to reconstruct and rethink frames for theories of action to distinguish the moral aspects of challenges beginning practition-ers face from the ways they thought about (or framed) the problems (i.e., Table 1.1), it became easier to distinguish social agency and issues related to students' navigation of education systems from the ways practitioners viewed the rules of the system.

Very frequently the issues that trouble beginning practitioners—and may motivate them to return to graduate school—are related to moral prob-lems that do not fit the rules of the system. Too often they feel that, because their suggestions were not followed, there was a problem with the system; too seldom do they engage in the process of reflecting on the reasons why the problems surfaced. Frequently, the development of new organizational ini-tiatives—including the top-down implementation of strategic plans—causes problems for practitioners in their work with students. When they try to voice student concerns, they feel rebuffed because of the focus on the rules of the system. I find it helps a great deal to have open discussion of these cases, to explore the system aspects as well as the personal, introspective aspects.

The friction between institutionalized, systemic views of problems and the human consequences of action does not disappear when professionals gain experience. For example, in a recent conversation with colleagues about our examination system, I raised issues that concern students and voiced some of the strategies they used to cope with our system (e.g., altering the timing of when they took exams). A colleague, an expert in student affairs, retorted by describing this as a problem with students "gaming the system." That set me back, because my point had been that the system we had was not working for students who did not fit our system owing to language, beliefs, or interests. After a while, I pointed out that we should think of the ways stu-dents navigate the system as positive, something we should encourage, rather than using the language of "gaming," which implies students were inappro-priately taking advantage of the system. At the core of this exchange, there were differing assumptions about the role of the rules of the system and the importance of students building their own academic capital to navigate and become successful (e.g., St. John et al., 2011). I am glad I found the courage to at least encourage public reframing of the problem.

My hope is this simple example and the previous discussion of Kim's case illustrate the role reflection on events plays in building the academic capital we need as professionals to move our academic system toward greater fair-ness when the rules are often exclusionary. In the case Kim used for class, the biased statement of a student leader could have led to exclusionary practices in student organizations if Kim had not spoken up. This same problem—the exclusionary effects of academic systems—was evident in the exchange I noted previously. Reflection on our own navigation within administrative discourses is crucial in moving systems toward greater fairness and equity. Kim actually changed the course of action by using her authority as a student affairs administrator. In the aforementioned case, I had to work in a collegial system in which I did not have the authority to make decisions. Instead, I realized that voicing critical issues was essential in the process of encouraging colleagues to act with greater fairness.

Collective Reflection on Action   Collective reflection on problem situations is more difficult than it might seem. Although people often espouse theories of justice, they often do not act that way. For example, the colleague who used the term *gaming the system* to disregard student choices about exam times had previously pushed through her version of a "social justice" program. Like the other curriculum systems of the department, the program was probably too rigid to achieve its purpose.

The underlying problem is that tinkering with the rules of the system does not solve the problems of injustice that emerge in practice. Typically, the missions and strategic plans of institutions promote social justice, but people in those systems often do not act in ways that are supportive of people marginalized by the system itself. I have argued that *communities of practice*— colleagues who work together to achieve greater fairness in admissions, curriculum, and instruction—are needed in educational systems; the analysis of evidence from a large number of case studies consistently confirms this hypothesis (St. John, 2009a, 2009b, 2013).

For example, in 1989–1990 at the University of New Orleans (UNO), I worked with Lou Miron, who, like me, was new to the doctoral program faculty, to revise the curriculum to take a more urban orientation and to recruit students from the city in addition to the suburbs that had been the traditional draw for the program. At the same time, we worked to hire three new colleagues who shared these commitments. The result was an urban-oriented leadership program that has been sustained by the university for decades, in spite of substantial faculty turnover.[1] Having a community of practice among faculty was essential to creating and sustaining an environment that could keep this program going during a five-year capacity-building period.[2]

Using Evaluation in Strategic Systems   Formative and summative evaluation research is also an important part of building capacity for change. Institutional data on applications, enrollment, student aid, and registration can be used to examine patterns of enrollment and persistence that inform institutional planning and budget decisions, including strategic planning. This approach has proven workable in a diverse array of colleges and universities in the Indiana Project on Academic Success (St. John, 2009a; St. John & Musoba, 2010). A similar approach can be used as part of an institutional research process.

For example, at the University of Michigan I worked with the College of Engineering (CoE) to use studies of enrollment and persistence to inform development of the STEM Academy (St. John, 2013). The CoE had a data-driven management approach. Research that examined challenges in retaining underrepresented students provided the basis for development of a new comprehensive approach to the bridge program (early courses on math) and support services.

Combining the use of data with the support of groups of faculty and administrators who are trying to innovate is key. That is, it is crucial to integrate an emphasis on critical reflection and community building in administrative practices with the use of a formal evaluation system. However, evaluation without reflection on practice rapidly becomes an external review process that stymies innovation rather than supporting and encouraging it.

Conclusion

Reflection on critical social challenges within colleges and universities is a crucial starting point for change in higher education that supports diversity. Although data can be used to assist transitional processes in educational reorganization, accountability often undermines the openness needed to engage in student-centered reform.

My proposal has been that we can use the methods of research and science to inform organizational adaptations that move educational systems toward fairer and more just practices that expand and equalize opportunities for diverse groups (St. John, 2013). I have worked in research partnerships over the past three decades to demonstrate this approach, but research is only one part of the process. Critical reflection on the social challenges that occur when we attempt to diversify learning environments is the starting point for change.

Student affairs professionals are on the front line of social change in higher education. If they do not take the time to reflect critically on their own practices—and, as a result of critical self-reflection, take steps to try out new approaches—it is unlikely our colleges and universities will become welcoming places for underrepresented groups. Building strong social systems that support students through their education involves networking, mentoring, and outreach. The development of formal systems to provide these support services is part of the solution, but we also need to critically reflect on and inform social action within higher education.

Notes

1. Evidence of continuation of this urban orientation was conveyed in an e-mail from Tammie Maria Causey, a professor at UNO, as part of an exchange about her ideas for a book in the Stylus series, Actionable Research for Social Justice in Education and Society.
2. In *Action, Reflection and Social Justice*, I analyzed praxis papers from five cohorts of students at UNO (St. John, 2009a). That text provided evidence on the development of an academic program focusing on social critical issues in education.

References

American College Personnel Association. (2006). Statement of ethical principles and standards. Retrieved from http://www.myacpa.org/au/documents/EthicsStatement.pdf

Argyris, C. (1993). *Knowledge for action: A guide to overcoming barriers to organizational change*. San Francisco, CA: Jossey-Bass.

Argyris, C., Putnam, R., & Smith, D. M. (1985). *Action science: Concepts, methods, and skills for research and intervention*. San Francisco, CA: Jossey-Bass.

Argyris, C., & Schön, D. A. (1974). *Theory in practice: Increasing professional effectiveness*. San Francisco, CA: Jossey-Bass.

Commission on the Skills of the American Workforce. (2007). *Tough choices, tough times: The report of the new commission on skills of the American workforce*. Washington, DC: National Center on Education and the Economy.

Gurin, P., Dey, E. L., Hurtado, S., & Gurin, G. (2002). Diversity and higher education: Theory and impact on educational outcomes. *Harvard Educational Review, 72*(3), 330–366.

Habermas, J. (1990). *Moral consciousness and communicative action*. Cambridge, MA: MIT Press.

Habermas, J. (2003). *Truth and justification*. Edited and translated by B. Fulmer. Cambridge, MA: MIT Press.

Hurtado, S., Milem, J. F., Clayton-Pederson, A. R., & Allen, W. R. (1998). Enhancing campus climates for racial/ethnic diversity: Educational policy and practice. *The Review of Higher Education, 21*(3), 279–302.

Kline, K. (2007). Professional development in student affairs: From learning about diversity to building just communities. In E. P. St. John (Ed.), *Confronting educational inequality: Reframing, building new understandings, and making change: Readings on Equal Education, Vol. 22* (pp. 314–348). New York: AMS Press.

Kohlberg, L. (1981). *The philosophy of moral development: Moral stages and the idea of justice*. San Francisco, CA: HarperCollins.

Kohlberg, L. (1984). *The psychology of moral development: The nature and validity of moral stages*. San Francisco, CA: Harper & Row.

Schön, D. A. (1987). *Educating the reflective practitioner: Toward a new design for teaching and learning in the professions*. San Francisco, CA: Jossey-Bass.

St. John, E. P. (2009a). *Action, reflection and social justice: Integrating moral reasoning into professional education*. Cresskill, NJ: Hampton Press.

St. John, E. P. (2009b). *College organization and professional development: Integrating moral reasoning and reflective practice*. New York: Routledge-Taylor.

St. John, E. P. (2013). *Research, actionable knowledge, and social change: Reclaiming social responsibility through research partnerships*. Sterling, VA: Stylus.

St. John, E. P., Hu, S., & Fisher, A. S. (2011). *Breaking through the access barrier: Academic capital formation informing public policy*. New York: Routledge.

St. John, E. P., Lijana, K., & Musoba, G. D. (2013). *Using action inquiry in education reform: An organizing guide for improving pathways from high schools through college*. Manuscript submitted for publication.

St. John, E. P., & Musoba, G. D. (2010). *Pathways to academic success: Expanding opportunity for underrepresented students*. New York: Routledge.

Yang, L. (2011). *World education finance and higher education access: Econometric analyses of international indicators and the implications for China*. Available from ProQuest Dissertations and Theses database. (UMI No. 3459080)

Yang, L., & St. John, E. P. (in press). Reframing the discourse of access: Three perspectives in viewing access in comparative higher education literature. In E. P. St. John, J. Kim, & L. Yang (Eds.), *Privatization and inequality: Comparative studies of college access, education policy, and public finance. Issues in globalization and social justice, Vol. 1*. New York: AMS Press.

2

ACTIONABLE KNOWLEDGE
AND STUDENT AFFAIRS

Megan Moore Gardner

A majority of student affairs practitioners are trained to reflect upon and use theory to inform practice. Once in the throes of demanding administrative work, however, reflection about theories in use when engaged in decision making may take a backseat to practical knowledge and situational experience. Hirsch (2000) described the disconnect from theory that often occurs for administrators by stating:

> Theories generated by researchers are developed under conditions that are far removed from the changing, dynamic circumstances of the practitioners' world. Researchers tend to write for one another and for graduate students who pull apart problems and examine them closely under controlled conditions. Administrators rarely read the research literature because they believe it is not written for them. From the standpoint of administrators, there is little room for research in the turbulent world of practice. The world of administrators has become increasingly fast paced, complex, and situational in an era of unprecedented accountability requirements and rapid change for institutions of higher education. There is little or no time for reflection, theory testing, or knowledge development. (p. 99)

A dilemma, then, often exists for those student affairs practitioners seeking to find ways of acquiring useful theory and research that may be applied in their daily work. Supplementing research and theories generated by "researchers" with those created by practitioners may result in scholarship that is applicable to current practice and that informs growth and change.

This chapter will introduce action research as a means for student affairs professionals to generate relevant and actionable research and theory in active and intentional ways. Student affairs professionals are called upon to be actively engaged in the research process in an effort to improve themselves

23

as well as the communities in which they live and work. Although action research was once considered a concept with questionable validity, it continues to emerge as an important research method that enables student affairs' practitioners to contribute to student learning and development and the betterment of higher education as a whole. This chapter discusses the essential components of action research, illuminates the many connections with student affairs work, and highlights the joint foci on informed learning and improvement to self and society.

What Is Action Research?

Action research is derived from a variety of academic disciplines, including sociology, education, and psychology; and its research presence is noted as early as the late 1930s, with the works of Kurt Lewin and with strong elements found in the philosophical work and experiments of John Dewey (Brydon-Miller, Greenwood, & Maguire, 2003; Minkler, 2004; Pain, 2004; van der Meulen, 2011).

Reason and Bradbury (2001) defined *action research* as

> a participatory, democratic process concerned with developing practical knowing in the pursuit of worthwhile human purposes, grounded in a participatory worldview which we believe is emerging at this historical moment. It seeks to bring together action and reflection, theory and practice, in participation with others, in the pursuit of practical solutions to issues of pressing concern to people, and more generally the flourishing of individual persons and their communities. (p. 1)

Action research posits that theory should emerge from practice. Van der Meulen (2011), concurred, stating, "An action research methodology is one in which theory can be articulated *through* and *in* action" (p. 1292). A type of research that bridges theory and practice and promotes action on the part of the researchers, action research embraces the notion that communities themselves are capable of identifying and conducting the research that is most valuable to them (Fals-Borda & Rahman, 1991; Reason, 1999; van der Meulen, 2011). When engaged in action research, practitioners work with others and fully participate in the design and implementation of the research process in an effort to generate the most meaningful results (Brydon-Miller et al., 2003; Pain, 2004; van der Meulen, 2011). The value of that theory, then, is found in its ability to be used for practice and toward the realization of individual and community well-being and positive social change (Brydon-Miller et al., 2003).

Actionable knowledge, which is composed of the theories, evidence, and tacit knowledge student affairs professionals use to inform their work and traverse the complex system of higher education, is produced and may be integrated into current professional practice. Such knowledge is garnered from the diverse array of experiences and backgrounds shared by not only the students with whom we work but also by our colleagues and peers within the field. Such diversity challenges us to reflect and incorporate a focus on continuous learning and development for practitioners in all levels of the student affairs/higher education enterprise. Additionally, action research serves a dual purpose of providing practical solutions for specific problems and of furthering theory and knowledge.

> This innovative form of research challenges the traditional notion that credible research should be objective and free of values. Rather, action research views knowledge as socially constructed and reflective of the values held by the communities in which the research is conducted and for whom the knowledge is generated (Brydon-Miller et al., 2003). Brydon-Miller et al. (2003) asserted that, "Action research rejects the notion of an objective, value-free approach to knowledge generation in favor of an explicitly political, socially engaged, and democratic practice" (p. 13). Complementing the "knowing through doing" concept of action research is the notion of working collaboratively with others in an effort to contribute to change in the organization, the community as a whole, and the researcher him or herself. "As action researchers reflect on their experiences, they acknowledge being profoundly changed by those experiences." (Brydon-Miller et al., 2003, p. 14)

Such research promotes and supports critical discourse and requires action on the part of the researcher who garners new knowledge through doing and reflecting. The focus on action to foster change is a key element that differentiates action research from other forms of inquiry. "A respect for people and for the knowledge and experience they bring to the research process, a belief in the ability of democratic processes to achieve positive social change, and a commitment to action, these are the basic values which underlie our common practice as action researchers" (Brydon-Miller et al., 2003, p. 15).

Action research stresses that tangible organizational and community benefits should be realized at the end of the process (Reason, 1999; van der Meulen, 2011). The emphasis on a process that results in such benefits results in solutions informed by a combination of "expert research and local knowledges" (Brydon-Miller et al., 2003, p. 25). Practitioners who feel that traditional methods of research are not relevant to their everyday organizational and community settings may find the philosophical and practical underpinnings of action research appealing and applicable to their work. Hirsch (2000) summed up the primary benefits of action research by stating, "Unlike traditional research in which theory, developed by the researchers or academics, is used to illuminate practice, participatory action research invites the practitioners to develop context-rich theories of their practice and then use these theories to effect change" (p. 102). Again, the goal is to produce "actionable knowledge" that can be directly used and woven into the fabric of daily practice.

Action Research and Student Affairs

As noted in preceding paragraphs, student affairs practitioners are typically trained to use theory and research to inform practice. Higher education/student affairs master's programs, more specifically, have diversified curriculums in recent years to incorporate a wider array of theories (e.g., cognitive-structural theories, human development theories, and postmodern writings); however, many continue to lack the inclusion of theories that intentionally promote critical discourse, encourage reflection, and stimulate social change (Kline, Moore Gardner, & Diaz, 2009). One means of facilitating such discourse, reflection, and change as well as to continue to bridge the gap between applicable theory and practice is through the incorporation of action research in both academic curriculums and professional practice (Hirsch, 2000). Such research will benefit both current and future student affairs professionals by promoting community-focused research, practical solutions, social change, and the development of meaningful professional praxis. This section will delve further into the connections between action research and student affairs, highlighting key concepts including professional praxis, reflection, and the continued need for increased commitment to social change in student affairs work.

Professional Praxis

There is a conscious commitment by many in both academic and professional settings to the promotion of moral and interpersonal development. This commitment is often demonstrated by the incorporation of student and cognitive development theories into academic curriculums and professional practices. What is frequently lacking, however, is a system that teaches professionals to act as social agents both inside and outside of the classroom. Action research can be used to inform professional praxis, which results in transformative development and change. Bell (1997) stated that practice is always shaped by theory, and theory provides a framework for questioning and challenging practices. Action research yields actionable knowledge, or knowledge that can actually be applied directly into practical experience. As such, the information resulting from such research does not just serve as a framework or guide; rather, it provides tangible practices and tools for direct application in the professional setting. Professional praxis, in turn, combines theory and practice to advance growth and promote change.

Professional praxis and action research are composed of many of the same fundamental ideas that make both concepts appealing to student affairs practitioners seeking to effect organizational and social change. Reflective of action research's focus on bridging theory and practice, praxis includes both theory and practice as "intertwining parts of the interactive and historical processes" (Bell, 1997, p. 4) that promote active learning and participation in discourse that reshapes learned belief systems. In many graduate programs and professional settings, theories are presented and used without reflection about or application to practical settings. In order to be agents of social change, current and aspiring student affairs professionals must understand how to effectively employ praxis techniques in academic, professional, and personal situations. Both professional and academic organizations must provide forums to discuss experiences and support the ability to develop professional praxis to ensure effective organizational and social change can be achieved (Kline et al., 2009).

It is not uncommon for graduate students and new practitioners to question how much seasoned practitioners actually incorporate and reflect upon the research and theories explored in graduate programs in their daily professional practice. Limited time and a laundry list of meetings, projects, and programs to attend to are but a few of the many obstacles practitioners face when trying to carve out time to truly think about how their work is informed by theory and research each day. Moving toward a model of professional praxis provides a means of helping professionals pause and reflect to enhance praxis without diverting extensive time and energy from other daily responsibilities. Once familiar with the idea and functions of reflection and professional praxis, professionals will be able to incorporate it seamlessly into their daily activity.

Reflection

Hirsch (2000) noted a lack of pertinent research available to inform practice and enhance critical discourse in student affairs practice. Similar to the obstacles to developing strong professional praxis, the author went on to argue that little time for reflection exists in the accelerated, accountability-driven world of higher education. Rather, professionals must rely on situational data and practical knowledge when making decisions and working to create organizational change. Reflection about learning contributes to the successful resolution of problems and can assist with the advancement of knowledge within a particular community. Further, what is learned through that reflection is not only important for the growth and development of the individual or group participating in that reflection. It is also important for any community stakeholders involved in research or the growth process.

Reflection is described in Leitch and Day (2000) as "a process or activity that is central to developing practices" (p. 180) and is highlighted in the action research literature as a necessary component of the process for promoting social change and development (Brydon-Miller et al., 2003; van der Meulen, 2011). Two types of reflective thinking, reflection on action and reflection in action, may be used by student affairs professionals when engaging in action research and/or working toward social change. Reflection on action is described as the "systematic and deliberate thinking back over one's actions" (Russell & Munby, 1992, p. 3), whereas reflection in action is "a way of making explicit some of the tacit knowledge embedded in action so that the agent can figure out what to do differently" (Argyris, Putnam, & Smith, 1985, p. 51). Additionally, Bell (1997) argues that reflection may be used as a tool to inform learning and practice. Combining reflection with action research offers the busy practitioner an opportunity to develop useable and applicable knowledge that informs professional praxis. Finally, reflection encourages "public learning" within an organization and provides forums for critical discourse within an organizational culture that is open to change (Ramaley, 2000).

Transformative Learning

Student affairs professionals have evolved throughout history from the keepers of in loco parentis to active facilitators of learning and development with students and other members of the higher education community. Most recently, effective student affairs professionals have been called upon to create engaging and transformative learning environments that encourage change for students and professionals alike. Transformative learning, according to Mezirow (2000), facilitates a change perspective that impacts how individuals make sense of events and experiences. Keeling (2004) espoused that "a transformative education repeatedly exposes students to multiple opportunities for intentional learning through the formal academic curriculum, student life, collaborative co-curricular programming, community-based, and global experiences" (p. 3).

Both *Learning Reconsidered* and *Learning Reconsidered 2*, added that a shift to transformative learning necessitates that student affairs professionals consider what facts and behaviors mean in relation to themselves, their organizations, and the communities in which they live and work (Keeling, 2004, 2006). Learning, from this perspective, is comprehensive and holistic, combining academic learning and student development.

Today, the perceived gap between academic and student affairs work has narrowed. Using a transformative learning approach, a more integrated model of learning and development in which student affairs professionals are thought to be more fundamental to learning because of the opportunities they provide students to learn through action, reflection, and engagement has emerged (Keeling, 2004, 2006). This focus on transformative learning is a natural fit with action research, because both share an emphasis on learning through action, reflection, useable knowledge, and individual and community learning and development. When coupled together, a transformative learning approach and action research can inform the development of effective professional practice and result in individual and community growth and change.

Social Change

As noted previously, action research emphasizes that organizational and community benefits should become a reality at the end of the process (Reason, 1999; van der Meulen, 2011).

The emphasis on social change incorporated into the action research model parallels the dimensions of the civic engagement outcome described in *Learning Reconsidered*. According to Keeling (2004), this outcome includes a "sense of civic responsibility, commitment to public life through communities of practice, engage[ment] in principled dissent, and effective[ness] in leadership" (p. 19). Student affairs practitioners who enact the principles highlighted by Keeling (2004, 2006) in their daily practice and use the skills both articulated in the transformative learning model and promoted in action research can integrate theory and practice, realize tangible benefits and solutions, and contribute to well-being and positive social change.

Schön's (1995) description of the unique action-based knowledge of the practitioner, which stated:

> When we go about the spontaneous, intuitive performance of the actions of everyday life, we show ourselves to be knowledgeable in a special way. Often we cannot say what we know. . . . Our knowing is ordinarily tacit, implicit in our patterns of action and in our feel for the stuff with which we are dealing. It seems right to say that our knowledge is in our action. And similarly, the workaday life of the professional practitioners reveals, in its recognitions, judgments, and skills, a pattern of tacit knowing-in-action (p. 29),

paralleled the ideas about a need for relevant practice-based knowledge and research set forth by Hirsch (2000) in the introductory paragraphs of this chapter. Jarvis (1999) concurred and argued that practitioners augment their understanding by learning; doing; thinking; and, finally, reflecting. An issue that may arise out of this "knowing-in-practice" is that learning becomes increasingly implicit and spontaneous, and opportunities to reflect upon what is occurring may be missed. This, then, further emphasizes the need for the development of strong professional praxis in order to promote and support regular reflection about theories and action in professional practice. Action research benefits student affairs practitioners seeking meaningful information, growth, and development, through its emphasis on coupling theory and practice with reflection and intentional community-focused discourse. As community-centered researchers of their own practice, student affairs professionals can use reflection to generate innovative knowledge and mend the traditionally disjointed relationship between research and practice.

Social Justice

Moving beyond a broad focus on social change to one that emphasizes social justice as a core value in student affairs work has proved necessary in a time of increasing economic stratification in society and in the microcosm of higher education (Friedman, 2005; Harvey, 2005; Huber & Stephens, 2001; Nussbaum, 2001; Sen, 1999). As access to higher education continues to increase, however, so, too, do the financial, social, cultural, and educational obstacles students now face. Postsecondary education is no longer a luxury that only a select few enjoy to prepare them for a few professions that require the two- or four-year degree. It is now a requirement for those seeking to earn a living wage and live a "comfortable life." Student affairs professionals, then, are faced with the challenge of helping students who have considerable challenges navigate the complex systems of higher education successfully.

Moreover, the move to a more globally competitive focus on both the societal and collegiate levels requires student affairs professionals to pause and reflect to ensure such focus results in a socially just, talent-development-focused postsecondary experience rather than a Darwinistic "survival of the fittest" type of culture. The movement away from a liberal arts education that opens the mind and informs the heart, for example, to one focused on science, technology, engineering, and math (STEM) fields in an effort to compete in the global market has significantly limited the opportunity for students to explore ideas and theories outside of their prescribed major fields. This is because of the rigorous field-based requirements that leave no time or room for courses in which students traditionally spent time discerning difference and thinking about the theory and tacit knowledge that informs how they see and interact with the world (St. John & Musoba, 2010). Rather, the in-class college experience is focused on gaining practical skills and technical information necessary to advance in the STEM fields. Although this is beneficial from the professional job placement and potential global success perspective, it minimizes the opportunity to engage in learning that contributes to social consciousness within higher education and society as a whole.

As discussed at greater length in the preceding chapter, student affairs professionals are now saddled with the challenge of moving toward a more socially just and diverse student but are often expected to do so within an organizational culture that remains tied to a history and tradition of elitism. This elitism continues to be manifested in the forms of ability, social status, and race, to name only a few, and plays a role in limiting true access to fair and just higher education for all members of society. In order to be the voice of the marginalized student within the tangled web that is higher education, student affairs professionals must have tools and theories that make sense with the demands and the general culture of today's higher education institution. It is no longer prudent to rely on methods informed by traditional notions of elitism and success. Professional learning through action research that produces actionable knowledge and tools for addressing current student and institutional issues will contribute to efforts to create dynamic and transformative learning organizations and more informed, socially just student affairs professionals.

Conclusion

The introduction of action research and actionable knowledge within the framework of student affairs provides useful tools to generate new knowledge, protect the voices of all of our students, and contribute to the growth and development of a transformative learning organization. Using such a model, student affairs professionals play an active role in the creation, testing, and integration of theories in their work. Learning in and through action promotes personal, organizational, and civic growth and augments professional praxis. Evident from a review of existing literature is the idea that action research complements the educational and organizational philosophies of student affairs practice and serves as an effective tool for practitioners seeking to create and use meaningful theory and research in daily practice.

References

Argyris, C., Putnam, R., & Smith, D. (1985). *Action science*. San Francisco, CA: Jossey-Bass.

Bell, L. (1997). Theoretical foundations for social justice education. In M. Adams, L. A. Bell, & P. Griffin (Eds.), *Teaching for diversity and social justice: A sourcebook* (pp. 3–15). New York: Routledge.

Brydon-Miller, M., Greenwood, D., & Maguire, P. (2003). Why action research? *Action Research,* 1(1), 9–28.

Fals-Borda, O., & Rahman, M. A. (Eds.). (1991). *Action and knowledge: Breaking the monopoly with participatory action-research*. New York: The Apex Press.

Friedman, T. L. (2005). *The world is flat: A brief history of the twenty-first century*. New York: Farrar, Straus and Giroux.

Harvey, D. (2005). *A brief history of neoliberalism*. New York: Oxford University Press.

Hirsch, D. (2000). Practitioners as researchers: Bridging theory and practice. *New Directions for Higher Education,* (110), 99–106.

Huber, E., & Stephens, J. D. (2001). *Development and crisis of the welfare state: Parties and politics in global markets*. Chicago, IL: University of Chicago Press.

Jarvis, P. (1999). *The practitioner-researcher: Developing theory from practice*. San Francisco, CA: Jossey-Bass.

Keeling, R. (Ed.). (2004). *Learning reconsidered: A campus-wide focus on the student experience*. Washington, DC: National Association of Student Personnel Administrators & American College Personnel Association.

Keeling, R. (Ed.). (2006). *Learning reconsidered 2: A practical guide to implementing a campus-wide focus on the student experience*. Washington, DC: American College Personnel Association, Association of College and University Housing Officers–International, Association of College Unions–International, National Academic Advising Association, National Association for Campus Activities, National Association of Student Personnel Administrators, and National Intramural-Recreational Sports Association.

Kline, K. (2007). Professional development in student affairs: From learning about diversity to building just communities. In E. P. St. John (Ed.), *Confronting educational inequality: Reframing, building new understandings, and making change, Readings on Equal Education, Vol. 22* (pp. 314–348). New York: AMS Press.

Kline, K., Moore Gardner, M., & Diaz, H. (2009, Summer). Fostering respect in the graduate classroom. *Academic Exchange Quarterly, 13*(2), 126–131.

Leitch, R., & Day, C. (2000). Action research and reflective practice: Towards a holistic view. *Educational Action Research: An International Journal, 8*(1), 179–193.

Mezirow, J. (2000). Learning to think like an adult: Core concepts of transformation theory. In J. Mezirow & Associates (Eds.), *Learning as transformation: Critical perspectives on a theory in progress* (pp. 3–34). San Francisco, CA: Jossey-Bass.

Minkler, M. (2004). Ethical challenges for the "outside" research in community-based participatory research. *Health Education and Behavior, 31*(6), 684–697.

Nussbaum, M. (2001). *Upheavals of thought.* Cambridge, UK: Cambridge University Press.

Pain, R. (2004). Social geography: Participatory research. *Progress in Human Geography, 28*(5), 652–663.

Ramaley, J. (2000). Change as a scholarly act: Higher education research transfer to practice. In A. Kezar & P. Eckel (Eds.), *New directions for higher education: Moving beyond the gap between research and practice in higher education,* p. 110. San Francisco, CA: Jossey-Bass.

Reason, P. (1999). Integrating action and reflection through co-operative inquiry. *Management Learning, 30*(2), 207–226.

Reason, P., & Bradbury, H. (Eds.). (2001). *Handbook of action research: Participative inquiry and practice.* London: Sage.

Russell, T., & Munby, H. (1992). *Teachers and teaching: From classrooms to reflection.* New York: Falmer Press.

Schön, D. A. (1995). The new scholarship requires a new epistemology: Knowing-in-action. *Change, 27*(6), 26–39.

Sen, A. (1999). *Development as freedom.* New York: Anchor Press.

St. John, E. P. (2013). *Research, actionable knowledge, and social change: Reclaiming social responsibility through research partnerships.* Sterling, VA: Stylus.

St. John, E. P., & Musoba, G. D. (2010). *Pathways to academic success: Expanding opportunity for underrepresented students.* New York: Routledge.

van der Meulen, E. (2011). Participatory and action-oriented dissertations: The challenges and importance of community-engaged graduate research. *The Qualitative Report, 16*(5), 1291–1301.

3

EVOLUTION OF A MORAL
AND CARING PROFESSIONAL

Kathleen M. Boyle

I n an effort to understand how professional student affairs and higher education educators integrate the constructs of justice and care, practitioners need an overview of the moral reasoning literature along with insights for integrating these constructs into daily practice. Educators in the field of student affairs and higher education ought to examine ways in which our practice, preparation programs, and professional role models reflect an integrated notion of justice in care (Gilligan, 1982; Noddings, 1984/2003). Working with undergraduate and graduate students, alumni, and colleagues all demands personal and professional contemplation of moral decisions and actions. This chapter connects the threads of theory, reflection, and justice and care ideologies with the evolution of moral and caring professionals who bring a focused action orientation into their daily practice.

Considering Moral Development and Defining Constructs

Moral reasoning is a basic component of moral education and development within a democracy. The overall goal of moral education is to produce thinking citizens for a democratic society by using a less direct educational approach and through enhancing judgments and reasoning (Zarinpoush, Cooper, & Moylan, 2000). In real life, not all issues fall neatly into domains of right and wrong. In many cases life issues overlap the two domains and thus demand high capacities in moral reasoning. In order to enter into and contribute to societal debates, people need not only to have clear definitions of related moral/social values and knowledge from more than one moral/social dimension but also to have strong capacities of moral reasoning. With these capacities, individuals will gain the ability to use that knowledge properly. Clearly, student affairs and higher education educators need to develop mature moral reasoning capacities side by side along with their students.

Having mature moral reasoning capacities, however, does not necessarily result in using those well-developed capacities in any situation. Many factors in our everyday lives can interfere with our reasoning capacities and affect the manifestation of them. Prior to moving forward into action, I would like to define several important underlying terms used throughout this work. Many of these terms arise from notions of philosophy and psychology that reach far beyond the purpose of this chapter—thus, what follows is a brief attempt to explain concepts that deserve a much more in-depth exploration.

Definitions

When moving into the arena of morality, researchers, theorists, and philosophers use several terms. Determining the foundations of ethics, moral development, moral reasoning, consciousness, care, the ethic of care, social justice, and social agency prepares educators to consider moving into personal development around issues of consciousness and deliberate action. *Ethics* or *moral philosophy* is a theory or system of moral values, a philosophy that involves systemizing, defending, and recommending concepts of right and wrong behavior (Fieser & Dowden, 2003/2009). *Moral development* represents "the transformations that occur in a person's form or structure of thought" with regard to what that person views as right or wrong, necessary or unnecessary (Kohlberg & Hersh, 1977, p. 54). *Moral reasoning* is "the cognitive component of moral behavior" (Evans, Forney, Guido, Patton, & Renn, 2010, p. 100).

In preparation for professional and personal action, exploring the constructs of consciousness, care, and deliberate action is also important. *Consciousness* arises from "the personal unfolding of ways of organizing experiences that are not simply replaced as we grow but subsumed into more complex systems of mind" (Kegan, 1994, p. 9). *Care* arises from interpersonal responsibilities and pro-social behavior (Sorkhabi, 2012). Gilligan (1982) differentiated between the notions of justice and care. The *ethic of care* rests on the principle that indifference and inaction do not harm the person in need and that someone responding who also does not experience harm acts to provide help (Gilligan, 1982). Noddings (1984/2003) explored practical ethics from the feminist perspective. Similar to Gilligan, she held that justice approaches are genuine alternatives to care approaches. Unlike Gilligan, Noddings (1994) was particularly interested in exploring the notion of "ethical caring—a state of being in relation, characterized by receptivity, relatedness, and engrossment" (p. 2). The construct of *social justice* finds its foundation with the principles of equality and solidarity. *Social agency* involves reacting from a place of being socially just, where the individual values human rights and recognizes the dignity of every human being. In a socially just society finding ways to create equality of opportunities and equality of outcomes are correspondingly important (Zajda, Majhanovich, & Rust, 2006).

When discussing issues surrounding social justice, distinguishing between the notions of a *deliberate action* as opposed to an *action* is important. *Deliberate actions* are those actions that a person does, not only intentionally, but also deliberately. Some may view these actions as "actions *par excellence.* An action of this sort is performed only when the person does something non-accidentally" (Foley, 1977, p. 59). The person "is not surprised to find that he [or she] has done this particular action and, moreover, he [or she] has, prior to the action, deliberated over the consequences of doing just this and not something else. Whenever a person acts deliberately, he [or she] brings about some event deliberately" (Foley, 1977, p. 59).

Exploring Theories of Moral Development

Over the years, psychological theorists and researchers established the domain of moral behavior by exploring several perspectives (Bore, Munro, Kerridge, & Powis, 2005). Freud (1930/1961) contemplated the ideas from the perspective of the psychodynamic conflict between the id and superego. According to Bandura (1977), moral behavior grew out of our social learning. Wilson (1975) explored moral behavior as evolved altruism. Currently, the dominant psychological theoretical lens of moral behavior is the cognitive developmental approach initially conceptualized by Piaget (1932/1965) and expanded by Kohlberg (1981, 1984).

Kohlberg's (1981, 1984) stage theory remains the standard lens regarding moral behavior after 30 years. He based his six-stage cognitive developmental progression of moral reasoning on a Kantian philosophy of morality as justice (Bore et al., 2005). Initially, people obey rules to avoid punishment or out of a sense of self-interest. They then move to meet others' expectations and societal norms. Finally, individuals develop an ability to use principled justice reasoning. Rational moral functioning directly arises from that justice reasoning (Kohlberg, 1981, 1984).

Many researchers acknowledge that the Kohlbergian framework does not account for the whole domain of moral reasoning, especially the domain of personal relationships (Kohlberg, Levine, & Hewer, 1983; Rest, Narvaez, Bebeau, & Thoma, 1999). Gilligan (1982) argued that differences in the moral reasoning of men and women were because of gender differences in moral orientation. She suggested men relied on a justice orientation and women on a care orientation (Gilligan, 1982). Lyons's (1983) research confirmed Gilligan's constructs of gender-related patterns of moral judgment—justice and care.

Building upon Gilligan's ideas and Lyons's confirmation, Stiller and Forrest (1990) supported the constructs with their research of undergraduate male and female residence hall students. Other studies found little support for such gender differences (Ford & Lowery, 1986; Jaffee & Hyde, 2000; Walker, 1984, 1989). Researchers noted that, when faced with "real-life" dilemmas, individuals use the orientations of both justice and care in moral reasoning. Jaffee and Hyde (2000) suggested that the most important predictor of moral orientation is, however, the type of dilemma, rather than gender.

Gilligan (1982) posited two gender-related moralities: *morality of justice*, centered on conflicting claims and individual rights; and *morality of care*, centered on responsibilities in relationships. Justice focuses on preventing violation of rules and principles issues, whereas care focuses on avoiding hurt and maintaining relationships. According to Gilligan (1982), the ethic of justice is inadequate to explain the care-oriented moral reasoning embedded in women's relationships.

Around the same time, educational philosopher Noddings (1984/2003) posited a notion she termed *the ethic of care*. Caring provides a foundation for ethical decision making. Noddings (2003) explored what she described as a "feminine approach to ethics and moral education" (p. 1). She claimed that philosophers have largely argued ethics "in the language of the father: in principles and propositions, such as justification, fairness, justice. The mother's voice has been silent" (p. 1). Building on the philosophical ideas of Sartre's "for-itself" and "in-itself," Heidegger's "being in the world," and Buber's "I-thou" and "I-it," Noddings (2003) identified two voices in relationship, one being the "one-caring" and the other being "cared for" (p. 4). She proposed a repositioning of education to encourage and reward not just logic, rationality, and trained intelligence, but also enhanced sensitivity and compassion in moral matters.

Human development reflects the progressive understanding of relational interdependence and how activities of care benefit both others and self (Gilligan, 1982; Noddings, 2003; Skoe, 1998). Skoe constructed and validated the developmental measure of care-based moral reasoning, the Ethic of Care Interview. The 1990s research established the proposed sequence with cross-sectional data (Skoe, 1998). Researchers identified that care reasoning correlated positively with such developmental indexes as role taking and complexity of reasoning (Skoe, Pratt, Matthews, & Curror, 1996); age, justice reasoning, and identity development (Skoe & Diessner, 1994; Skoe & Marcia, 1991;

Skoe & von der Lippe, 2002); and women's androgyny (Skoe, 1995; Sochting, Skoe, & Marcia, 1994).

Others have developed theories for exploring moral reasoning and development. Each of these theorists (well known in the disciplines of student affairs and higher education) continues to build on the work of others. At the same time, each extends into ways adults construct moral decision making and notions of moral reasoning.

Theory and Practice in Student Affairs and Higher Education

Building on Piaget's (1932/1965) assumptions of stage-related development, educational philosopher Dewey's (1933, 1938/1960) concepts about reflective thinking, and Kohlberg's (1981, 1984) work on cognitive and moral development, King and Kitchener (1994) created the Reflective Judgment Model (RJM). At the core of their research, King and Kitchener wanted to know, How do people decide what they believe about vexing problems? The foundation of the RJM was Dewey's notion that people make reflective judgments in order to bring closure to uncertain situations. Individuals move from not reflecting at all (relying on authorities to help them make decisions), to a place where knowledge is uncertain or contextual and subject, and finally find themselves reflecting and recognizing that knowledge is constructed and can be supported with reasoned arguments. The researchers made several suggestions to faculty and student affairs educators, placing particular emphasis on respect for perspectives and withholding judgment about developmental progress (King & Kitchener, 1994).

A theorist who regarded the intertwining of developmental realms, Kegan (1982, 1994, 2000) argued that both cognitive and affective components are involved in meaning-making processes. Kegan's (1994) theory proposed "the evolution of consciousness, the personal unfolding of ways of organizing experiences that are not simply replaced as we grow but subsumed into more complex systems of mind" (p. 9). His theoretical constructs evolved from "stages of development" in 1982 to "orders of consciousness" in 1994, finally referring to "forms of mind" in 2000 (Evans et al., 2010).

Of particular note to student affairs educators, Kegan suggested "the relationship or fit between what contemporary culture demands of our minds and our mental capacity to meet those demands has specific application to the realm of work" (Brendel, Kolbert, & Foster, 2002, p. 217). He further argued that such demands from contemporary culture represent a qualitatively more complex "form of mind" and thus require an even greater caution on the part of those who would make these demands of others. Faculty who prepare professionals in the academic disciplines of counseling and education (i.e., counselors, teachers, student affairs educators, etc.) need to heed these claims and reflect on the ways in which a form of mind perspective "has significant implications for preparation programs devised to equip professional helpers for roles in various settings with diverse populations" (Brendel et al., 2002, p. 217). Professionals in each of these human services areas must be capable of critical self-reflection to create new frames of reference for contemplating the world and constructing meaning from each of their work or practical experiences (McAuliffe & Eriksen, 1999).

Similarly, Sprinthall (1994) noted an urgent need for professional preparation programs at the graduate level (counseling, student affairs, etc.) to focus on a developmental model. Analogous to Schlossberg, Waters, and Goodman's (1995) constructs about transitions and Noddings's (1984/2003) notions of dialogue, Sprinthall (1994) proposed that a rich sequence of change marks adult development: a dialectic process involving a series of transformations of moving through the contradictions of previous assumptions to a synthesis or integration of the old and the new. Higher levels of psychological development in adults predict successful functioning in multiple areas related to serving others as an advisor, a supervisor, or a counselor, including greater empathic communication, more autonomy and interdependence, more flexible counseling and teaching methods, and a reduction in prejudice (Holloway & Wampold, 1986; Peace, 1995; Rest & Narvaez, 1994; Sprinthall & Thies-Sprinthall, 1983; Stoppard & Miller, 1985).

Emerging from this discussion of theoretical foundation is important. Although this provides a foundation for the exploration, the heart of this discussion needs to center around deliberate action. How do professional educators challenge themselves to move beyond discussing theory and movement into practice? When does deliberate action come alive in the work that we attempt to accomplish in our daily lives?

Moving From Theory to Practice—Evolution of a Caring Professional

With each new day, higher education and student affairs educators face dilemmas that require deliberate action and understanding a variety of perspectives. At the same time, today's educators struggle with determining how best to identify their own progress and development while moving toward the goals of providing an open space where ideas, experiences, and dialogue can flow. Noddings (1994) suggested that moral learning occurs through conversations in the context of caring relationships. She also referred to "what may be the very heart of moral education—the quality of ordinary conversation" (p. 114), in which we regard our dialogue partners more highly than the topic being discussed. When people open a space to dialogue, ideally they start by devoting time to shared values including respecting, trusting, and honoring the dignity of the other engaged in that dialogue (Healy & Liddell, 1998). Healy and Liddell identified that if we can create this place and/or space, "we can engage our differences" (p. 42).

Noddings averred, "Insistence on respect and loving regard leaves us open to influence; we are pledged to learning and exploring together, not to a total transmission of moral values" (1994, p. 116). Dialogue, or what Healy and Liddell (1998) called "developmental conversation," allows for mutual exploration, which, in turn, creates a "dynamic experiential opportunity for moral, cognitive, and emotional growth" (p. 42). Healy and Liddell determined that the developmental conversation implies a commitment to Rogerian thinking, and thus

> would require us to develop conversations to facilitate the relational self. Such a conversation implies a commitment to Rogerian thinking and assumptions about the helping relationship: that one should hold the other in unconditional positive regard; that empathy is valued; that the relationship is built on sincerity, authenticity, and therefore risk taking. Such conversations, like all educational interventions, may be remedial or developmental; however, the conversation assumes a willingness to learn from one another, to be engaged in the moment with students, to maximize their readiness to learn. (p. 42)

Noddings (1994) also noted that "moral educators can also profit from a consideration of conversation in our own interactions" (p. 117). She referred to the way in which "our attention shifts from judgment to action, from justification to motivation" (p. 117). Being willing to engage in "ordinary conversation" is at the heart of moving oneself toward moral interactions with others. If we cannot converse, how can we even hope to move toward understanding and meaningful interaction?

This level of conversation does not simply occur by identifying opportunities to "chat" with our friends, peers, and colleagues. Intentionality is at the heart of these interactions. The Jesuits (an order of Catholic priests) identify one of the core tents of their values is to be "contemplatives in action" ("Jesuit Writes About," 2011). When functioning as a contemplative in action, individuals reflect prior to moving into action (an essential part of the reflection for the Jesuits includes prayer). As professional educators, engaging in interactions where we take the time to step into a quiet space to think before, during, and after action is important when addressing the needs of those with whom we work.

We communicate respect and value for the other involved in the dialogue and interaction when we reflect prior to reacting—this is particularly important when dealing with any issues involving social justice. Lawrence-Lightfoot (2000) researched ways in which we communicate respect for one another through our interactions. She noted "respect creates symmetry, empathy, and connection in all kinds of relationships, even those . . . commonly seen as unequal" (pp. 9–10). She recognized that respectful relationships maintain their qualities and reproduce themselves. In her research, Lawrence-Lightfoot identified "six windows on respect—*empowerment, healing, dialogue, curiosity, self-respect,* and *attention*"—and went on to describe each one, revealing a different point of view and offering a variety of insights into various experiences.

Practicing Moral and Caring Actions

Deliberate intentionality is an important consideration for student affairs educators when combining reflection with action. Yet, many might express incredulity at what they perceive to be an impossible stance in our field. How can anyone be a deliberate actor or a contemplative in action when she or he finds herself or himself "putting out fires" and reacting to the real or perceived immediate needs of various groups (students, supervisors, parents, administrators, etc.)? At times situations demand an immediate response (e.g., physical assault or verbal abuse, a parent on the phone, a supervisee responding to his or her supervisor). Yet, even within these circumstances, being deliberate in your actions is possible, particularly if you have reflected and prepared yourself to respond. Acting deliberately, from a place of reflection, or as a contemplative in action requires that the professional agrees with the importance of this perspective and puts these ideas and constructs into practice *prior* to facing the most current pressing need, issue, or concern.

When developing a notion of being a contemplative in action, acknowledging the involvement of both the intellect and the spirit is vital (Fejfar, 2006). When discussing the Ignatian or Jesuit construction of contemplatives in action, Fejfar suggested that contemplation must be based on love. "The intellect moves the will to act. Whether love motivates one to act or the will motivates one to act, the result is the same, contemplation finds its fulfillment in action which carries out the results of contemplation. . . . This is called infused contemplation" (Fejfar, 2006, pp. 1–2).

Working within college and university settings, student affairs and higher education educators find themselves attending to many constituent groups. Each of these groups (students, parents, supervisors, administrators, faculty, alumni, etc.) brings with them idiosyncratic ways of conceptualizing their needs and wants. Student affairs and higher education educators need to construct an individual "portfolio" of understanding and work toward improvement in each area:

- Understanding that different cultures is not only an important consideration for welcoming a diverse student body, but also for welcoming the cultures within various constituent groups;
- Knowing who you are and reflecting on your own stage of development within various psychosocial, identity, cognitive, and moral realms (Chickering & Reisser, 1993; Gilligan, 1982; Kegan, 1994; King & Kitchener, 1994; Kohlberg, 1984; Noddings, 1994); and
- Anticipating moral dilemmas that you may face in your position.

How have you challenged yourself to understand those who hold different identities from your own? Each of us who has the honor of working with other human beings needs to undertake an assessment of our own privilege and oppression. Even when desiring to "do good," the potential for harm increases when educators do not intentionally reflect on language and perspective through the lenses of privilege and oppression.

One important consideration is reflecting on your own developmental stage prior to moving into these discussions with others. Are you ready to reflect on and discuss issues of ethics, moral development, moral reasoning, care, the ethic of care, social justice, and social agency? If not, how can you challenge yourself (or request others to challenge you) toward further development? When discussing their final vector of development, Chickering and Reisser (1993) referred to a sequential process of three overlapping stages to *developing integrity*:

- *Humanizing values*: shifting away from automatic application of uncompromising beliefs and using principled thinking in balancing one's self-interest with the interest of one's fellow human beings.
- *Personalizing values*: consciously affirming core values and beliefs while respecting others' points of view. In this stage, an individual undertakes principled reasoning and displays behavior that follows suit.
- *Developing congruence*: matching personal values with socially responsible behavior—that is, truly behaving in alignment with what one believes. The individual's stances are based on thoughtful reflection and are clear to others. (pp. 236–237)

In essence, you need to purposefully think through and reflect on the question, "Who am I?" The result of this contemplation should be an incorporation of values and corresponding actions that are likely to create a sense of consistency of being (Healy & Liddell, 1998). Healy and Liddell (1998) contend that this consistency of being is necessary for authentic moral leadership to occur.

How will you deliberately open up Lawrence-Lightfoot's (2000) "windows" and offer empowerment, healing, and an occasion for dialogue; communicate curiosity; develop self-respect in another; and pay attention to the individual commanding your respect? Whether you are dealing with a roommate conflict, intervening with intragroup conflict within student government, approving an event sponsored by students, or responding to a parent, supervisor, or administrator, you have a chance to consider your response. If you are not intentional in your actions and contemplative with regard to moving into, through, and out of conversations and/or interactions, you will miss this opportunity to be a contemplative, reflective, ethical, caring, and moral practitioner.

Conclusion

Recognizing daily opportunities to act is an essential part of being a caring professional. We must push ourselves to experience life through a lens of caring and approach our work with an ethic of care and work from a stance of being contemplatives in action. Kegan (1994) addressed the concern that contemporary professions are making "more a claim on the mind than a demand for the acquisition of particular skills" (p. 178); what he has called a claim for "a way of knowing" (p. 185). The complexity of the role of the student affairs professional continues to evolve. The personal integration needed by a student affairs educator to be emotionally available for genuine empathic intervention, to be able to respond appropriately yet differentially to student needs, and to serve as an advocate for equality and justice is a function of the higher stages of cognitive complexity. According to Sprinthall (1994),

> [I]f the task at hand involves complex human relationship skills such as accurate empathy, the ability to read and flex, to select the appropriate model from the professional repertoire, then higher order psychological maturity across moral, ego, and conceptual development is clearly requisite. (p. 96)

Not only do graduate preparation programs and site supervisors need to teach graduate students how to apply theory to the undergraduate students with whom they work; educators must contemplate their own development and preparation for dealing with dilemmas faced throughout higher education. Restructuring graduate preparation programs to promote student affairs educators' cognitive and moral development must be a priority to meet the prevailing demands of a compelling and challenging profession.

References

Bandura, A. (1977). *Social learning theory*. Englewood Cliffs, NJ: Prentice-Hall.

Bore, M., Munro, D., Kerridge, I., & Powis, D. (2005). Not moral "reasoning": A Libertarian–Communitarian dimension of moral orientation and Schwartz's value types. *Australian Journal of Psychology, 57*(1), 38–48.

Brendel, J. M., Kolbert, J. B., & Foster, V. A. (2002). Promoting student cognitive development. *Journal of Adult Development, 9*(3), 217–227.

Chickering, A. W., & Reisser, L. (1993). *Education and identity* (2nd ed.). San Francisco, CA: Jossey-Bass.

Dewey, J. (1933). *How we think: A restatement of the relation of reflective thinking to the education process*. Lanham, MD: Heath.

Dewey, J. (1938/1960). *Theory of the moral life*. New York: Holt Rinehart Winston.

Evans, N. J., Forney, D. S., Guido, F. M., Patton, L. D., & Renn, K. A. (2010). *Student development in college: Theory, research, and practice* (2nd ed.). San Francisco, CA: Jossey-Bass.

Fejfar, A. J. (2006). *Jesuit spirituality: To be a contemplative in action*. Retrieved from http://www.scribd.com/doc/540/Jesuit-Spirituality-To-Be-a-Contemplative-in -Action

Fieser, J., & Dowden, B. (Eds.). (2003/2009). *Ethics*. Internet Encyclopedia of Philosophy. Retrieved from http://www.iep.utm.edu/ethics/

Foley, R. (1977). Deliberate action. *The Philosophical Review, 86*(1), 58–69.

Ford, M. R., & Lowery, C. R. (1986). Gender differences in moral reasoning: A comparison of the use of justice and care orientations. *Journal of Personality and Social Psychology, 50*, 777–783.

Freud, S. (1930/1961). *Civilization and its discontents*. New York: Norton.

Gilligan, C. (1982). *In a different voice: Psychological theory and women's development*. Cambridge, MA: Harvard University Press.

Healy, M. A., & Liddell, D. L. (1998). The developmental conversation: Facilitating moral and intellectual growth in our students. In M. A. Healy & J. M. Lancaster (Eds.), *Beyond law and policy: The role of student affairs. New Directions in Student Affairs* (No. 82), pp. 39–48. San Francisco, CA: Jossey-Bass.

Holloway, E. L., & Wampold, B. E. (1986). Relation between conceptual level and counseling-related tasks: A meta-analysis. *Journal of Counseling Psychology, 33*(3), 310–319.

Jaffee, S., & Hyde, H. S. (2000). Gender differences in moral orientation: A meta-analysis. *Psychological Bulletin, 126*, 703–726.

Jesuit writes about "contemplatives in action" found along US/Mexican border. (2011, December 28). *Jesuits: National Jesuit News*. Retrieved from http://www.jesuit.org/blog/index.php/2011/12/jesuit-writes-about-contemplatives-in -action-found-along-u-s-mexico-border/#more-4881

Kegan, R. (1982). *The evolving self.* Cambridge, MA: Harvard University Press.

Kegan, R. (1994). *In over our heads: The mental demands of modern life.* Cambridge, MA: Harvard University Press.

Kegan, R. (2000). What "form" transforms? A constructive developmental approach to transformative learning. In J. Mezirow (Ed.), *Learning as transformation* (pp. 35–69). San Francisco, CA: Jossey-Bass.

King, P. M., & Kitchener, K. S. (1994). *Developing reflective judgment: Understanding and promoting intellectual growth and critical thinking in adolescents and adults.* San Francisco, CA: Jossey-Bass.

Kohlberg, L. (1981). *The philosophy of moral development: Moral stages and the idea of justice: Vol. I. Essays on moral development.* San Francisco, CA: Harper & Row.

Kohlberg, L. (1984). *Essays on moral development: Vol. II. The psychology of moral development.* New York: Harper & Row.

Kohlberg, L., & Hersch, R. (1977). Moral development: A review of the theory. *Theory Into Practice, 16*(2), 53–59.

Kohlberg, L., Levine, C., & Hewer, A. (1983). *Moral stages: A current formula and a response to critics.* Basel, NY: Karger.

Lawrence-Lightfoot, S. (2000). *Respect: An exploration.* New York: Basic Books.

Lyons, N. P. (1983). Two perspectives: On self, relationship, and morality. *Harvard Education Review, 53,* 125–145.

McAuliffe, G. J., & Eriksen, K. P. (1999). Toward a constructivist and developmental identity for the counseling profession: The context-phase-stage-style model. *Journal of Counseling and Development, 77,* 267–280.

Noddings, N. (1984/2003). *Caring: A feminist approach to ethics and moral education.* Berkeley, CA: University of California Press.

Noddings, N. (1994). Conversation as moral education. *Journal of Moral Education, 23,* 107–118.

Peace, S. (1995, November 19). *Promoting the development of mentor and novice counselors: Applying theory to practice and research.* Paper presented at the 1995 International Conference of the Association for Moral Education, Fordham University, New York.

Piaget, J. (1932/1965). *The moral judgement of the child.* New York: Free Press.

Rest, J. R., & Narvaez, D. (Eds.). (1994). *Moral development in the professions: Psychology and applied ethics.* Hillsdale, NJ: Erlbaum.

Rest, J. R., Narvaez, D., Bebeau, M. J., & Thomas, S. J. (1999). *Postconventional moral thinking: A neo-Kohlbergian approach.* Mahwah, NJ: Erlbaum.

Schlossberg, N. K., Waters, E. B., & Goodman, J. (1995). *Counseling adults in transition* (2nd ed.). New York: Springer.

Skoe, E. E. (1995). Sex role orientation and its relationship to the development of identity and moral thought. *Scandinavian Journal of Psychology, 35,* 235–245.

Skoe, E. E. (1998). Ethic of care: Issues in moral development. In E. E. Skoe & A. L. von der Lippe (Eds.), *Personality development in adolescence: A cross-national and life-span perspective* (pp. 143–170). London: Routledge.

Skoe, E. E., & Diessner, R. (1994). Ethic of care, justice, identity and gender: An extension and replication. *Merrill-Palmer Quarterly, 40*, 109–117.

Skoe, E. E., & Marcia, J. E. (1991). A care-based measure of morality and its relation to ego identity. *Merrill-Palmer Quarterly, 37*, 289–304.

Skoe, E. E., Pratt, M. W., Matthews, M., & Curror, S. (1996). The ethic of care: Stability over time, gender differences and correlates in mid- to late adulthood. *Psychology and Aging, 11*, 280–292.

Skoe, E. E., & von der Lippe, A. L. (2002). Ego development and the ethics of care and justice: The relations among them revisited. *Journal of Personality, 70*, 485–508.

Sochting, I., Skoe, E. E., & Marcia, J. E. (1994). Care-oriented moral reasoning and prosocial behavior: Question of gender or gender role orientation? *Sex Roles, 31*, 131–147.

Sorkhabi, N. (2012). Caring reasoning in interpersonal relationships: Cognition about moral obligation and personal choice. *North American Journal of Psychology, 14*(2), 221–244.

Sprinthall, N. A. (1994). Counseling and social role taking: Promoting moral and ego development. In J. Rest & D. Narvaez (Eds.), *Moral development in the professions: Psychology and applied ethics* (pp. 85–100). Hillsdale, NJ: Erlbaum.

Sprinthall, N. A., & Thies-Sprinthall, L. (1983). The teacher as an adult learner: A cognitive view. In G. Griffin (Ed.), *Staff development: Eighty-second yearbook of the National Society for the Study of Education* (pp. 13–35). Chicago, IL: University of Chicago Press.

Stiller, N. J., & Forrest, L. (1990). An extension of Gilligan's and Lyons' investigation of morality: Gender differences in college students. *Journal of College Student Development, 31*, 54–63.

Stoppard, J. M., & Miller, A. (1985). Conceptual level matching in therapy: A review. *Current Psychological Research and Reviews, 4*, 47–68.

Walker, L. J. (1984). Sex differences in the development of moral reasoning: A critical review. *Child Development, 55*, 677–691.

Walker, L. J. (1989). A longitudinal study of moral reasoning. *Child Development, 60*, 157–166.

Wilson, E. O. (1975). *Sociobiology: The new synthesis. Cambridge*, MA: Belknap Press of Harvard University Press.

Zajda, J., Majhanovich, S., & Rust, V. (Eds.). (2006). *Education and social justice.* Dordrecht, The Netherlands: Springer.

Zarinpoush, F., Cooper, M., & Moylan, S. (2000). The effects of happiness and sadness on moral reasoning. *Journal of Moral Reasoning, 29*, 397–412.

PART TWO

CONCRETE TOOLS AND SAFE SPACES FOR PRACTICING DIFFICULT DIALOGUES IN PROFESSIONAL PRACTICE

4

CRITICAL SOCIAL DIALOGUES AND REFLECTING IN ACTION

Shakira Henderson and Kimberly A. Kline

As I sat in the chair waiting for my class to begin, I looked down at the desk in front of me, where a seemingly bored student had sat previously. I say he or she was bored because he had taken the liberty to leave a stylishly written and profound message inked into the wooden laminate. In what I could immediately recognize as medium-point black Sharpie was written, "Minds are like parachutes . . . they only function when open." Following the statement was drawn a cartoonish young man jumping out of an airplane to his peril. It seems he took this course because his mind and parachute were unfortunately closed. On the desk, close to the edge, the artist (or vandalizing criminal, depending on how one chooses to view the situation) drew the poor young man's brain decorated with a peace sign and his (now useless) open parachute. Later, I would find out that the quote was taken from Sir Robert Thomas Dewar, a Scottish physicist, but at the time it seemed to me that this unknown graffiti artist had written it to me as a new lens through which to view the dialogues that were taking place every week in class. This class, entitled Moral Reasoning in Higher Education, focused on introducing students to the lexicon of moral reasoning in higher education. It tied in the importance of critical social dialogues, as well as themes of social justice/agency, which culminated in two major projects for the semester.

My experiences within the class will serve in this chapter as a structure through which to explore effective approaches to critical dialogues and "difficult" conversations among students currently in higher education preparatory programs. They will also show the possible positive outcomes of students who are encouraged to reflect on action about their current roles within their professional lives. This would ideally move toward honing the skill of reflection in action. This opportunity to become skilled in reflection in action serves as a pathway through which students can begin to formulate their professional praxes, which should, at least in part, advocate for social justice. I will then examine how higher education preparatory programs can benefit by providing a required social justice/agency–oriented course as a way to supplement internships and graduate assistantships. This course will be a benefit by training students to become reflective practitioners (Schön, 1983). This means that as students are experiencing real-life professional situations, they put into practice the theories they learned while in their social justice–oriented course.

Moral Reasoning in Higher Education and Critical Dialogues

At the time that I attended the program, the Moral Reasoning in Higher Education course was an elective. The class, which was slated for the 7:30 p.m. to 10:10 p.m. time slot during the spring semester, was dialogue driven and loosely structured. The first half of the class focused on reading and analyzing St. John's (2009) text *College Organization and Professional Development.* There was a particular emphasis on what St. John cites Schön as calling *case statements* (a tool for reflective practice) (St. John, 2009, p. 77). In these case statements, we were provided with a model for students to follow in one of the practice exercises. In the assignment, our professor urged students to follow this model and describe a conflict that occurred in their professional lives. Following the background information, we were assigned to separate the page into two sides. On the left side, we would write the dialogue that ensued between all parties involved in the conflict. On the right, we would write a reflection of how we responded to the event. St. John (2009) says, "Graduate professional education should introduce students to reflective practice and to the difficulty of enacting openness within communities of professional practice" (p. 76). By doing the case statement exercises, framing them, openly discussing them in group settings, and practicing these new skills, students are able to become more comfortable with discussing difficult issues in class and translating those gains into their current professional experiences, such as internships and graduate assistantships. We were assigned this task as an exercise in examining our motivations and framing our assumptions. This would be one of the tools to aid us in building and eventually articulating our own professional praxis.

The following is an example of my case statement for the class:

Shakira is an orientation leader (OL) at a large research university in the western New York area. This orientation program runs from May through August and uses students as mentors and tour guides for the upcoming year's freshman class. Two staff members as well as two undergraduate students, called *team leads*, supervise the Orientation Leader Program. The culture of this particular orientation program is one in which the orientation leaders are encouraged to fraternize with each other outside of work hours. Orientation leaders are required to stay in the residence halls while students are visiting and are strongly encouraged to stay and participate in team-building activities during the times the freshmen are not on campus. Shakira is a good orientation leader and has received only positive feedback, but last week, in passing, one of the team leads questioned why she never hangs out with the rest of the staff.

After one orientation-closing meeting, Shakira's team lead pulls her to the side to talk to her for a moment about the perceived alienation.

Participants

Shakira (S), orientation leader

Timothy (T), team lead of the orientation staff

Dialogue	Reflection
(T1) Hey, Shakira! I've been meaning to talk to you this week, but we've all been so busy. I wanted to let you know how great of a job you're doing with the students.	*I know that's not even what he wants to talk to me about. It's 6 p.m. on the last day of this session; I want to go home.*
(S1) Thanks, Tim, I really appreciate it. What's up?	*I'm trying to give him an opening to get to the point.*
(T2) We missed you at the trip to the Science Museum last Saturday; where were you?	*I'm going to be nice and tactfully answer. But I really feel like it's none of his business where I am on my own personal time, when I'm not supposed to be working.*
(S2) I was at my apartment; I had to wash clothes. Plus I had already made plans with some friends who also stayed on campus for the summer.	*I gave a valid reason for missing it; maybe now he'll drop the conversation. I'm a senior; I have real friends. I cannot understand why they expect me to become best friends with coworkers*
(T3) Well, that's not the only thing. We've noticed that you're rarely around. I never see you in the lounge. It seems like you are alienating yourself from the rest of the team. I'd hate to see it affect how you work together during the actual sessions.	*I honestly don't think I did anything wrong, and he's being condescending. I do my job well, and I'm honestly offended that he would imply otherwise*
(S3) Honestly, I feel like the lines of professionalism are blurred. I've never gotten any complaints about my quality of work, but right now, I'm being reprimanded for not hanging out with the rest of the team on my free time.	*I'm just going to stick to a completely professional work argument, and I can't lose.*

(Continues)

Dialogue	Reflection
(T4) Orientation is a special beast, and to work well and relate well with the students you need to have a relationship beyond a professional one. We don't want you to come off as insincere. I mean, I know you genuinely want to be here, but come on, you don't even stay in your room, which, by the way, is against the rules.	*I can't believe this! How can he tell me what I can do on my own personal time? I need this recommendation, so I won't give him a piece of my mind. I'll explain my part and leave it at that.*
(S4) I'm on campus when the students are here. I pay rent to live in the on-campus apartments; I'd like to use it. Plus I'm a senior; I have friends already. I feel like I'm being punished for having a life outside of orientation.	*Everything about my body language has changed and become defensive. I'm not discussing this further. I hope he doesn't stereotype me as an aggressive black girl.*

My case statement addressed assumptions I had about the roles of employees and employers, assumptions I made about the age and maturity of my supervisor, and the fear of assumptions that would be made about me based on race and gender. By using "case statements as a window on theories of action," we were able to put into practice what St. John (2009) refers to as "a three stage process of building reflective practice skills" (p. 76). The three stages of this process are creating case statements, analyzing these statements within revised frames in group dialogue (reflection on which ways one's own actions relate to specific replicating patterns of action; see St. John, 2009, p. 78), and practicing new strategies by using action experiments. These action experiments are the essential piece that links theory to professional practice for master's or doctoral students in higher education administration preparatory programs.

On the due date of our first assignment, my classmates and I arrived with our completed case statements, unsure of what to expect of the discussion that would take place. During class, our instructor split us into small groups to give us the opportunity to discuss our conflicts within the paradigms, the replicating patterns of action, or revised frames. During these discussions, the class embarked on meaningful and open critical dialogues and facilitated frank discussions concerning social justice/action and diversity or multicultural awareness, in addition to explorations of our roles as burgeoning professionals. We spent considerable time facilitating "difficult" or "touchy" conversations with each other and later moved on to reflecting on ways that we could use our newly learned skills to have the same types of conversations on and off college campuses. According to St. John (2009), "The process of developing skills in reflective practice parallels the process of acquiring expertise. Reflective skills can be learned through reading, reflection, and actions that involve trying new practices. . . . When members of organizations have skills in open critical reflection, it is easier to engage in initiatives involving collaborative action inquiry" (p. 13). Engaging in open critical reflection about our professional lives led us as a class to examine our attitudes and assumptions that permeated into other aspects of our lives and identities. Creating an open space where it is okay to question one's own and others' motivations and commitments regarding social justice allowed the class to make the appropriate connections between one's own core beliefs and values and our (at the time unarticulated) professional praxis. It also explored diversity and multicultural awareness outside of a class entirely devoted to that and related those types of discussions to professional life. By making "diversity" pervasive in my program's curriculum and making it a component of every class, the graduate program at my institution made a bold statement about the importance of emphasizing deep, meaningful exploration of the topic.

The moral reasoning class was composed of a diverse representation of people across race, ethnic group, sexuality, and age. However, it was fairly homogenous in terms of gender (there were only four males) and socioeconomic status (most people in the class ranged from working poor to middle class in their backgrounds). It was in the midst of this ideal incubator that we began to work toward purposely creating an environment conducive to achieving the goals of practicing reflection on action and having open critical dialogue. During the semester some strategies used within the class were successful and some were not, but overall this class is a model for strategies that can be used to accomplish these goals.

Several important factors made this class a model for such strategies:

- Building rapport among students and instructors
- Achieving what Avery and Steingard (2007) call political trans-correctness, through the combination of maintaining authenticity and sensitivity and not creating pressure for students to self-censor, which will create an optimal zone of understanding
- Being clear and intentional with the language that is used in the class and in writing assignments
- Being compassionate and, as a part of growth toward the second half of the class, moving beyond microlevel compassion to being social agency–oriented

Building Rapport Among Students and Instructors

Building rapport among students and instructors was important because an environment of mutual respect and comfort was the foundation upon which we could build a milieu conducive to open critical dialogue. During our moral reasoning class, our instructor would often have us sit in a circle, which promoted inclusivity (Torres Santos, Ottens, & Johnson, 1997) and did not allow students to shrink away or hide from the conversation by sitting toward the back or corner of the room. Also we would begin the class by going around the circle and responding to a conversational topic. It could be anything ranging from something positive we did that day to something in the news that concerned us. Although initially some students were hesitant to participate in the opening comments, this strategy was effective because it served as a testing ground for the openness and trustworthiness of the group. It allowed students to witness a group of their peers who are open, honest, friendly, and nonjudgmental about topics unrelated to diversity and social justice. This made students more likely to feel comfortable sharing their writings and opinions about more sensitive subjects.

Striving Toward Political Trans-Correctness Within the Classroom and Using Intentional Language

There is a climate of self-censorship among students in courses dedicated to social justice, diversity, and multicultural awareness. Students, for fear of retaliation, are hesitant to express any views counter to popular ideologies and political correctness. Avery and Steingard (2007) surmise:

> Insincere politically correct comments undermine pedagogical learning objectives in diversity education in two ways. First, they prevent authentic personal sharing of the real and oftentimes intense issues related to diversity. Second, because of this lack of meaningful sharing, politically correct contributions impair or neutralize collective learning about diversity. (p. 270)

One solution to these issues is to create an environment geared toward *political trans-correctness*. When I use the term *political trans-correctness*, I am referring to Avery and Steingard's (2007) model for the integration of authenticity (being genuine to beliefs that may in fact be polarizing) and sensitivity (purposefully trying not to offend anyone based on race, gender, ability, sexuality, religion, class, or any other perceived societal difference). At the intersection of these two ideas lies the *zone of understanding*, where the most can be gained from social justice– or diversity-oriented dialogues (Avery & Steingard, 2007).

In our moral reasoning class, we encouraged authenticity by constantly emphasizing the value of individual voice, even if that voice is not in agreement with the standard narrative for "political correctness." During the semester I was enrolled in the class, we were able to witness and discuss the media frenzy surrounding the killing of African American teen Trayvon Martin. Much of our conversation centered on the role of race in the media as well as in the judicial system. Often during discussions students would cite media sources that espoused views countering what was politically correct. Our instructor responded to this type of input by emphasizing the importance of not taking away anyone's voice, regardless of whether or not we agreed with it. By experimenting first through using media topics as a centerpiece of discussion, students who had varying opinions became more confident in expressing those opinions, because they witnessed their classmates' constructive (not reactive) responses to the opinions of those outside of the classroom setting.

Being Clear and Intentional With the Language That Is Used in the Class and Writing Assignments

Although we sought to avoid political correctness to the point of mindless self-censorship, we were able to maintain sensitivity by being encouraged to be clear and direct in our words and writing. Language does matter. We emphasized the use of inoffensive neutrally charged terms and reinforcing our own personal opinions with some type of independent research. By emphasizing this, our instructor ensured a nonoffensive climate, but still encouraged students to present their authentic truths. By being encouraged to share their truths, other students in the class who may have agreed with these students but were too afraid to be demonized for their beliefs had a learning opportunity. Because they presented their beliefs, the entire class was able to critically analyze them, whereas had we not maintained sensitivity and authenticity we would have missed out on a number of ample learning opportunities.

Being Compassionate and Moving Beyond Compassion Toward an Orientation of Social Justice/Agency

Compassion for one's fellow human beings is at the core of any move toward social justice/agency and giving these ideas a primary role in higher education administration courses. Compassion is manifested on multiple levels of a higher education professional's job, regardless of which job he or she works. As a professional, it is important to promote caring for the individual lives and concerns of all students as well as faculty and staff on college campuses.

For graduate students, compassion is an important safeguard against expressing one's authentic ideas using offensive or inappropriate language. This model for compassion within higher education is important, but, in order to engage as active world citizens, it is imperative that we move beyond compassion on the micro level of individual interactions and move toward compassion in a broader sense. This means a move toward social justice and eventually social agency.

Although we used case statements to address the assumptions we held about the workplace, the instructor also used the ensuing class dialogue about the assumptions to drive the class toward thinking in terms of social agency. In the second assignment of the semester, we were asked to split the class into two groups, examining a social issue related to higher education. After this examination, we were to formulate a critical action research project with the first group presenting using the medium of film/video and the second group using the medium of photography. As a class, we had a lot of discussion surrounding the fact that the achievement gap in K–12 education is affecting the realm of higher education in terms of student preparedness and ways in which we were socially responsible for helping the situation.

We approached the subject on the most basic level, by engaging in a dialogue with at-risk students who participated in a local after-school program. We opened the dialogue by asking the question, What do you know about college? What we gained from the dialogue was that, although many of the students were of age to begin the college application process, the majority of them knew very little about institutes of higher education other than common cultural tropes surrounding college drinking and fraternity and sorority hazing. They were unfamiliar with even the most basic financial aid jargon and knew very little about things like what factors go into choosing an institution of higher education or choosing a major once one arrives there. While engaging in dialogue with the students and framing their responses for use in our critical action research projects, we provided them with a few resources on how to begin their journey toward higher education. Among each other and with the students we emphasized that socioeconomic status and race should not be a determining factor in whether or not a child is equipped with the tools to pursue higher education. Although we were ambitious in our goals for the action project, there was a lot to be desired in terms of effective social agency. This was primarily because of the time constraints of the class. True social agency in this arena would require a major commitment of time and energy from university members (students, faculty, and staff) interested in sustaining long-term change. Despite this, we did gain experience in using our roles as higher education students and professionals to impact at least a small change for at-risk students, by providing them with resources to learn more about applying to and attending college.

We were able to use our experiences with the critical action research project as fodder for further dialogues about diversity, inclusion, and social justice while in class. The Moral Reasoning in Higher Education course was positive in that it used a number of strategies that encouraged critical dialogues about difficult subjects. By practicing this skill every week in class, students were equipped with ways to translate these skills into their professional lives. However, the class fell short of this goal in two areas. The first was in having too broad a focus in "social agency"; because we were the first group of students to concentrate on this area of higher education and social agency, we approached the action project using trial-and-error procedures. The primary errors we made were in not setting clearly defined objectives for our critical action research project and not following up after the class to formulate ways of sustaining social agency to effect positive change for these young students. The second area where we fell short was in often slipping into lazy surface examinations of "diversity" on college campuses. We all advocated for diversity and multiculturalism, but often did not take the time to explore what that truly meant or what the implications of that impetus were for higher education. This is where we must move beyond a surface exploration of isms to a place that offers deeper insight into who we are as burgeoning professionals. This requires a reevaluation of how we as student affairs professionals view diversity and multiculturalism. We are at the juncture between diversity/multicultural awareness and the goal of moving beyond reflection on action to reflection in action. This is the birthplace of the idea for making such a social justice–oriented class—much like the Moral Reasoning in Higher Education class that I described—a required supplement to internship courses or students' graduate assistantships in higher master's and doctoral programs.

Reevaluation of Diversity and Multiculturalism in Higher Education

Although my experiences in this class were overwhelmingly positive, we would often rely on overgeneralizations and unclear expectations of diversity. Acceptance of diversity was somewhat of a mantra within our master's program. This blanket use of the term *diversity* is evident not only within the higher education program at the school I attended, but also in the media. If one were to search Google Scholar for the phrase "Diversity in higher education" in scholarly journals published in 2012, one could come up with hundreds of examples. This extensive use of the term has in a way blurred what it means to prepare a competent workforce of student affairs professionals. It is now commonplace for the term *diversity* to pop up in multiple facets of higher education. Diversity offices aimed at highlighting different cultures exist on many college campuses. Diversity training aimed at creating a more tolerant student body and staff might be offered. And many admissions offices make vague references to diversity as a selling point for why students and their families should come to their particular campus. But what does this mean for future practitioners within the field? Many of these measures ensure that preparatory programs include the *idea* of acceptance of "others," but do not explicitly create a clear objective or action. Is diversity to be treated as a competence one should acquire, or an idea to be encouraged? Or is it an issue that should be dealt with?

A number of publications are available for faculty, staff, and graduate students in the area of multicultural competence (e.g., Pope & Reynolds, 1997) and multicultural awareness, and scores on multicultural knowledge (e.g., King & Howard-Hamilton, 2003) and multiple identities (e.g., Gayles & Kelly, 2007). The topics of privilege (e.g., Castellanos, Gloria, Mayorga, & Salas, 2007; Lechuga, Clerc, & Howell, 2009) and models of oppression (e.g., Edwards, 2006; Freire, 2002; Kivel, 2002) are the focus of many scholarly articles.

Although these publications are noteworthy, they overlook the professional development of higher education and student affairs practitioners-in-training. Students learn about theories, identities, ways of knowing, and research on college students and administration but do not have ample opportunities to reflect on and integrate those theories into practice (Nottingham, 1998). In many cases, social justice issues are treated at an espoused level, but insufficient attention is given to the *practice* of social justice and social agency education in student affairs administration. To understand and resolve this dilemma, it is important to focus on research that creates paths toward actionable change within higher education and student affairs doctoral programs.

Social Justice–Oriented Classes as a Part of the Core Curriculum

The inclusion of a social justice–oriented class in the core curriculum of higher education administration master's programs creates a positive channel for these questions to be turned into solutions aimed at social justice. The inclusion of this type of class goes beyond the benefits of simply having different people working together and speaks directly to cultivating the National Association of Student Affairs Administrators' (NASPA) and the American College Personnel Association's (ACPA) core competency of equity, diversity, and inclusion. NASPA and ACPA purport that on a basic level, student affairs practitioners should be able to facilitate dialogue effectively among disparate audiences, demonstrate fair treatment to all individuals, change aspects of the environment that do not promote fair treatment, and analyze the interconnectedness of societies worldwide and how these global perspectives impact institutional learning (ACPA & NASPA, 2010). Moral reasoning and social justice classes are the ideal educational environments in which to gain the skills to effectively master these competencies. When these types of courses are used as supplements to professional experiences such as internships or graduate assistantships, they can be even more effective.

Moral reasoning and social justice–oriented classes can give students the opportunity to hone the skill of what Schön (1983) calls reflective practice. *Reflective practice* is defined as the ability to focus on beliefs and values that inform an individual's actions. The individual then uses this same focus to inform further action. This skill is essential to developing expertise and can be practiced via strategies such as role playing but can be better developed while on the job. A social justice–oriented course taken as a supplement to an experiential learning experience allows students to make the ideas of diversity, multiculturalism, and social justice within their professional lives more tangible. It creates an environment where a group can commit to engaging in open dialogue about the conflicts surrounding diversity and inclusion at work. This is an opportunity for students to practice what they learn in theory, while under the security of an internship—a position designed for learning and making mistakes.

Although history, counseling, and student development theory provide much of the framework for most higher education preparation programs in the United States (Herdlein, Kline, Bouqard, & Haddad, 2010), internship courses serve as arenas of experiential learning for graduate students. Many of these internship courses are geared toward a lot of reflection on action but very little reflection in action. This is because, despite students' reinforcement of theory while in classes, many of the seasoned professionals who are supervisors to students may not engage in office or departmental policies that complement the strategies the students are learning in their classes. These mixed messages can potentially lead students to believe that the strategies for equity, inclusion, and diversity that they are learning about in class are not necessary for success in the workforce. In actuality, this idea is very far from the truth. For example, if a student fulfilling an internship in the athletics office encounters a difficult conversation centering around diversity or multiculturalism, and he or she is not enrolled in a supplemental social justice class, who is there to guide the student so that he or she will know how to address similar discussions in his or her future professional life? How can we rely solely on what is taught in core classes like The History of Higher Education Administration and Student Development Theory if diversity, equity, and multiculturalism are treated as subsections of student affairs and not wholly integrated within a student's experience in a higher education graduate curriculum?

Unintentionally, higher education and student affairs administration programs that omit moral reasoning/social justice classes from the core curriculum or from the entire curriculum can reinforce the message being sent to their students that what they are learning in theory differs from what they will actually use in practice. Higher education master's and doctoral students who are engaged in some type of experiential learning alongside enrollment in a social justice–oriented class will benefit most from being able to practice the skills of reflecting in action on what they learned about diversity and multiculturalism. They will also benefit from the class being a safe space to practice critical dialogues about difficult issues and learn strategies for engaging in those same types of discussions in professional situations.

References

ACPA College Student Educators International & NASPA Student Affairs Administrators in Higher Education. (2010). *Professional competency areas for student affairs practitioners*. Washington, DC: Author.

Avery, D., & Steingard, D. (2007). Achieving political trans-correctness: Integrating sensitivity and authenticity in diversity management education. *Journal of Management Education, 32*, 269–293.

Castellanos, J., Gloria, A., Mayorga, M., & Salas, C. (2007). Student affairs professionals' self-report of multicultural competence: Understanding awareness, knowledge, and skills. *NASPA Journal, 44*(4), 643–663.

Edwards, K. E. (2006). Aspiring social justice ally identity development: A conceptual model. *NASPA Journal, 43*(4), 39–60.

Freire, P. (2002). *Education for critical consciousness*. New York: The Continuum Publishing Company.

Gayles, J. G., & Kelly, B. T. (2007). Experiences with diversity in the curriculum: Implications for graduate programs and student affairs practice. *NASPA Journal, 44*(1), 193–208.

Herdlein, R., Kline, K., Boquard, B., & Haddad, V. (2010). A survey of faculty perceptions of learning outcomes in master's level programs in higher education and student affairs. *College Student Affairs Journal, 29*(1), 33–45.

King, P., & Howard-Hamilton, M. (2003). An assessment of multicultural competence. *NASPA Journal, 40*(2), 119–133.

Kivel, P. (2002). *Uprooting racism: How white people can work for racial justice*. Gabriola Island, BC: New Society.

Lechuga, V., Clerc, L., & Howell, A. (2009). Power, privilege, and learning: Facilitation encountered situations to promote social justice. *Journal of College Student Development, 50*(2), 229–244.

Nottingham, J. E. (1998). Using self-reflection for personal and professional development in student affairs. In W. Bryan & R. Schwartz (Eds.), *New directions for student services: Strategies for staff development: Personal and professional education in the 21st century* (pp. 71–81). San Francisco, CA: Jossey-Bass.

Pope, R. L., & Reynolds, A. L. (1997). Student affairs core competencies: Integrating multicultural awareness, knowledge, and skills. *Journal of College Student Development, 38*, 266–277.

Schön, D. (1983). *The reflective practitioner: How professionals think in action.* New York: Basic Books.

St. John, E. (2009). *College organization and professional development: Integrating moral reasoning and reflective practice.* New York: Routledge.

Torres Santos, J. R., Ottens, A. J., & Johnson, I. H. (1997). The multicultural infusion process: A research-based approach. *Counselor Education and Supervision, 37*(1), 6–18.

5

THE GAME CHANGERS

Moving Beyond Isms to Restore Civility to the Academy

Wanda M. Davis

We can no longer simply conduct research and talk about isms and the academy. We must move to a practical level of application and create safe spaces where critical dialogue, self-reflection, and personal responsibility take place. Action must be taken to build a culture of civility and caring. Campus crime reports and security logs indicate that physical and verbal acts of violence and intolerance that cause harm to another person have become all too familiar (Almedia, 1993; Scribner et al., 2010). These data provide information on the nature of campus violence and help us to identify the perpetrator and the likely victim. Every area of the campus is vulnerable. Although the academy has no duty to protect the community from the violence of a third party, taking no action to minimize the risk clearly makes the campus environment unhealthy and unsafe. No longer is it acceptable to only offer programs and services that are geared toward the victim. Colleges and universities must be proactive and also design initiatives that target the perpetrator.

Once we realize that most acts of violence go unreported and that issues and problems of the broader culture become ambient factors in the university community, the question then becomes, how can institutions of higher education provide a safer campus environment? How do we take back our campuses and control for violence? This is especially important as the larger society struggles with the very same concerns. Legal complexities and matters involving due process simply compound the problem. It is clear that in the academy, antisocial behavior that is based in violence and intolerant behavior must be addressed. National and international occurrences on campus; pressing economic, political, and social forces; and compelling events have always affected and will continue to affect higher education (Davis, 2012; Davis & Dulski, 2001; Sandeen & Barr, 2006). Our campuses are not isolated, and

65

there is more than one way to respond to harmful, disruptive, selfish, belligerent, and inconsiderate behavior. It is critical, however, that we acknowledge the problems that we face and to respond appropriately and decisively with structured programs that bring about civility. We must begin to work with those perpetrators who show a readiness to grow and help them learn about respecting themselves and others.

This chapter is presented in three parts. The first section provides a working definition of violence followed by a survey of current literature, setting the appropriate conceptual framework for successful implementation of educational interventions. Then we discuss identifiable targets of violence on college campuses and their likely perpetrators. As game changers, we must understand the basic assumptions, goals, educational objectives, and minimal standards required for any administrative application, recognizing that it will not happen overnight. We must work successfully with those who show promise of becoming productive citizens but need to learn to control their behavior and how to not willfully hurt others in the process. Therefore, we end with a discussion of the major components of an educational intervention that provides a template for implementation.

Toward a Working Definition

Volumes of research exist on campus violence. In the last decade alone this topic has been studied intensely by student affairs professionals, counselors, legal scholars, and academics. This vast body of knowledge provides a clear picture of the status of violence in higher education and highlights current trends. The study of violence is extensive because we understand the destructive nature of violence and acts motivated by intolerance, particularly after colleges were forced to provide hard data as a result of the Cleary Act and other legislation. The current rise in criminal acts on college campuses includes off-campus violence that in some cases has resulted in death (Davis, 2007; Langford, 2004; Lederman, 1994, 1995; Office of Postsecondary Education, 2008, 2012). However, most research focuses on the victim and that is not enough. Not in these days and times. We must move toward intervention with the perpetrator as the main focus if we want the threat to stop. We need to change the game.

How we define violence is extremely important to our discussion. For our work, *violence* is defined as behavior that is intended to hurt another person and is the antithesis of student development (Roark, 1987). It includes physical violence, interpersonal violence, institutional violence, intellectual violence, courtship violence, hazing, the violent use of sex, and ethnoviolence. Committed acts of violence such as sexual assault; homicide; hate crimes that include race-, ethnicity-, sexual orientation–, and gender-based motives; rioting; arson; and bombing are also included (Cantalupo, 2009; Davis, 1998; Drysdale, Modzeleski, & Simons, 2010; O'Neil, 1989; Reynolds & Von Destinon, 1993; Roark, 1994b). Hazing on campus, including the realms of athletics, Greek life, and military training, are included as well as nonintimate rape, stalking, and nonsexual assault. In today's world, we must also add bullying, sexual harassment, cyberstalking, and cyberharassment along with intimate partner acts of violence that include rape and homicide (Paludi, 2008). We also understand that, in the case of sexual violence, a man attacking a woman is treated differently than a woman attacking a man. This historical gap, as it relates to gender, is no reason for acts of violence to be committed against men. Through same-sex or heterosexual relationships, women can commit battery also. *Intimidation*, as part of this conversation, is "to unlawfully place another person in reasonable fear of bodily harm through the use of threatening words or other conduct, or both, but without displaying a weapon or subjecting the victim to actual physical attack" (Family Educational Rights and Privacy Act, 1974).

This widely framed definition of *violence* is useful for two reasons. First, it reflects the breadth and depth of thinking and research on the topic. Second, it highlights the truly violent nature of many of the harmful student behaviors that student affairs professionals come across in their work, with shootings and killings being less frequent. It forces student affairs professionals to think critically about policy and how they define and respond to campus violence (Hemphill, Roberts, & LaBanc, 2010; Shang & Stevens, 1988).

To shed light on the legal complexities involved, one might ask, What happens if a student has been charged but not convicted of a crime? Snow and Thro (1994) examine this issue in the case of *Nero v. Kansas State University*, wherein an accused perpetrator remains on campus pending trial on a sexual assault charge and commits a second violation prior to the hearing. Snow and Thro's work provides a solid rationale for interventions designed specifically for the accused. Both Stith, Jester, and Bird (1992) and Palmer (1993) performed similar studies that provide insight into the minds of those who commit violent acts, and, although their findings are very important, they, too, concentrate on the victim, with little discussion on interventions directed toward the perpetrator. Additionally, both studies have a limited sample size. Banyard, Moynihan, and Crossman (2009) speak to reducing sexual violence and discuss the role of student leaders as empowered bystanders, treating violence on college campuses in a general fashion. The relevance of this information is not in question, but the existing literature has generally looked at these issues in isolation and do not allow us to look across types of violence to gauge the relative prevalence and context. Nor do they introduce intervention processes. As game changers, we must do more to reduce the issue of power and control and take the campus back.

Targets of acts of violence and intolerance are well documented by the U.S. Secret Service, U.S. Department of Homeland Security; the Office of Safe and Drug-Free Schools, U.S. Department of Education; and the Federal Bureau of Investigation, U.S. Department of Justice (Drysdale et al. 2010). Other researchers offer insight on various forms of violence as seen on campus and offer prevention and solution strategies for law enforcement professionals, faculty, staff, parents, and students (e.g., see Nicoletti, Spencer-Thomas, & Bollinger, 2001). Yet, as they indicate, one can only imagine how many go unreported. We need a comprehensive approach to addressing this epidemic, and we need it now.

One of the most complex and perplexing issues on the American college campus as it relates to violence is diversity and institutional responsibility. A critical study traced incidents or tensions related to race, gender, and sexual orientation over a three-year period, 1994–1996. The data was analyzed by region and suggests that assessment be used as a strategy for systematically gauging campus climate and culture across the academy. Using *The Chronicle of Higher Education*, the study determined the number of incidents that were related to race, gender, and sexual orientation; where they were occurring; and who the targets of the tension were (Davis, 1998). To gain a deeper understanding of the offenders, victims, circumstances, and university or college response, Bromley (2005) also used the *Chronicle* and explored articles from 1989 to 2001 for incidents of campus murder. Both Davis and Bromley highlight the fact that college campuses share commonalities with the community at large. For example, with regard to murders, Bromley found that as in the general population, domestic, intimate, and workplace violence were present in campus homicide cases. In a majority of the cases studied, there was some relationship between the offender and the victim, and both tended to be members of the campus community as students, faculty, or staff. Bromley suggests that you must assess whether the identified individual possesses the intent and ability to carry out an attack against a member or members of the community and if the perpetrator has taken any steps to prepare for the attack (Bromley, 2005). Both Davis and Bromley agree that you must manage the threat posed by the individual to include disrupting potential plans of attack, mitigating the risk, and implementing strategies to facilitate long-term resolution.

Other researchers present firsthand accounts of those who have lived through a violent incident and continue to deal with its aftermath. Topics cover violence, suicide prevention, and mental health promotion, and a number of the authors offer suggestions about how to create campuswide systems and emergency plans to address campus violence by providing strategies for addressing institutionally appropriate and sensitive ways to achieve healing and recovery (Hemphill et al. 2010; Reynolds, Roark, Shang, & Stevens, 1988).

The Victim

Students as well as graduate teaching faculty are usually the targets of student shootings, causing the entire campus environment to be affected by the trauma left behind (Bromley, 2005). Five groups appear to experience the most frequent and serious acts of violence. A survey of 49 colleges and universities in 30 states, covering approximately 141,000 students, identifies (a) women; (b) racially or ethnically recognized students, particularly those students of color; (c) nonheterosexual students; along with (d) religious groups, such as Muslim and Jewish students, as the most frequent victims (Palmer, 1993). Palmer's research is important because it also identifies (e) the resident assistant as a common target of violence—a fact that directors of residence life have known and possibly neglected for years. Five general types of incidents have been identified: self-inflicted, partner or dating, residential community, members of out-groups, and unknown others. There are also those who will commit violence against themselves by way of self-destructive behaviors, including alcohol or drug abuse, eating disorders, or suicide (Orzek, 1989). Others help us to understand that partner or dating violence manifests itself through verbal insults, physical slapping, punching, or rape. The residential community may experience violence that includes harassment, stealing, hazing, intimidation, and vandalism. Members of racial and unidentified sexuality groups usually experience a combination of the mentioned forms of violence.

Although most studies concentrate on the historically White campus (Davis, 1996; Office of Postsecondary Education, 2008, 2012), we know that this violence is universal to all campuses, including today's minority-serving institutions. Although race may not be the dominant motivator, as stressed, the need for campus safety and prevention affects the entire system of higher education. Basically, the same issues are a burden across the academy. Hayes contends that prevention lies with the community and that an educated community is more effective in prevention than an uneducated one. Again, Hayes's study focuses on the victim rather than on those who commit the acts, yet his comments speak volumes for the entire campus community (Hayes, 1993, 1994). And, although Meggett (1994) examines environmental factors that affect African American college and university students, the thrust is in prevention programs for minority males and their families on the topic of violence and drug abuse (Davis, 1996). Meggett examines the need for an intervention for violent offenders; however, there is no provision of a model for intervention.

Fortunately, there is some discussion of solutions to the problem. Experts in law, human resources/employment policy, psychology, criminal justice, and education offer sage, real-world advice to campus administrators, parents, students, and employees on how to prevent and manage campus violence. Paludi (2008) offers insight into the reasons behind violent acts and presents prevention and therapeutic techniques that students can use to protect themselves. Paludi addresses the legal responsibilities of schools, as well as the psychological fallout on people in the aftermath of violence. Featuring interviews with student-victims and providing sample policies and training programs, this work helps students learn how to spot situations of potential violence, helps faculty in the use of classroom exercises to raise awareness with the goal of violence prevention, and assists college administrators as they learn how to safeguard the people and assets in their care (Paludi, 2008).

Incidents of shootings on campuses such as Virginia Tech and the irresponsibility of Penn State and other institutions bring issues surrounding campus violence to the forefront once again. Historically we know that the academy has always suffered from problems with stalking, sexual harassment, bullying, rape, robbery, burglary, and intimate partner violence, among other things. In fact, the incidence rates of campus violence are quite startling. For example, the incidence of sexual harassment among undergraduate students ranges between 20 and 80 percent each year (Drysdale et al. 2010). Between 8 and 15 percent of college women say they have been raped (Banyard et al. 2009; Potter, Moynihan, & Stapleton, 2011). We must stop the violence, and the most difficult of all dialogues rests with the perpetrator.

The Perpetrator

In order to design interventions targeted toward the accused, it is valuable to construct a description of those most likely to commit violent acts on campus, because some groups are more prone to commit violence than others. Using Reynolds's (1989) conceptualization of all violence as oppression, we understand that violence is often committed by members of privileged groups. Hence, victimization of historically oppressed groups as studied by Palmer becomes understandable but certainly unacceptable (Palmer, 1993). Palmer notes that when a member of a group is victimized, the perpetrator has usually focused upon gender, race, ethnicity, religion, sexual orientation, or authority figures as it relates to job duties. These data help us to understand that historically most violence committed against women is perpetrated by men and that most violence committed against nonheterosexual students is perpetrated by heterosexuals. Particular to the African American community, issues of sexual harassment or assault, violence toward women, and sexual orientation are generally overshadowed by the issue of race; the code of silence surrounding these hurtful attacks is alarming (Davis, 1998).

Hazing is another common form of violence on campuses. For our purposes, *hazing* is defined by Roark (1987) as a violation of the common rules of decency. Hazing commonly occurs in groups such as athletic teams and Greek organizations and other groups that perform initiations on their new members. Roark (1990) writes, "People are at their best and worst in groups." Hazing of any kind certainly portrays the college and university community at its worst. It is apparent, however, that very little has been written on what to do with the perpetrator once an offense has been committed.

Aggregated data from 2010 clearly indicates that intimidation and simple assault continue to rise at alarming rates and that race, sexual orientation, gender, and religion remain the dominant targets of violence both on and off campus. Race is the number one factor (Office of Postsecondary Education, 2012). But, charting the trends alone does not provide us with solutions that address this negative and hurtful behavior (Davis & Richbart, 1998). Violence by students in the academy is aggressive and more violent. Guns are involved in more than one third of all violent student crimes, and in most cases, the perpetrators who shoot to kill are White males (Hutchinson, 2007). More often than not, they are socially isolated, frustrated, and want to settle a grudge, usually with a professor or a failed sexual encounter, or in response to failure in a love relationship with another student.

An earlier study looks at the academy and traces incidents or tensions related to race, gender, and sexual orientation over a three-year period (Davis, 1998). These data are analyzed over nine regions as identified by the Bureau of the Census. The major questions examined were: How many incidents related to race, gender, and sexual orientation were published by *The Chronicle of Higher Education* over a three-year period? Where did they occur? and who were the targets?

A look at the total campus of students, faculty, and staff suggests that failure to assess individual campuses and higher education as a whole will undoubtedly leave America at a loss. This author also suggests that if we do not understand the complexity of higher education and how diversity affects the system as a whole, we are doomed to continue to provide educational environments that fall prey to civil animosity, misunderstanding, and suspicion (Davis & Richbart, 1998). Current research supports this conclusion

(Drysdale et al., 2010). This is not to say that there has been no progress toward attaining diversity and the eradication of campus violence; however, this chapter is written with the understanding that, on the whole, American higher education has yet to achieve a place in society and in the world where it can ignore the fact that incidents of tension and violence continue to occur on our campuses. This is particularly harmful because the majority of these incidents relate to race, gender, and gay-lesbian populations.

Violence Prevention

Three levels of violence prevention are presented in the classic work of Mary L. Roark (1987). The first level is *tertiary prevention*, which is limiting the damage of violence and victimization that has already taken place through services for the victim. *Secondary prevention* is identifying existing problems and bringing about effective correction before further damage occurs. *Primary prevention* is preventing new cases of violence by addressing its causes and adjusting variables relating to the conditions that foster it. In addition, Reynolds, Lustgraaf, and Bogar (1989) address several specific options that institutions can execute to reduce and prevent violence on their campuses. Roark (1988) offers a guide for preventing campus violence. Focusing on violence prevention, assessment, and planning, Roark provides five components that violence prevention efforts are likely to include. First, they raise awareness and knowledge. Second, they develop policies and procedures. Third, they implement educational programs for skill development and attitude change. Fourth, they serve the needs of past victims. And fifth, violence prevention models must change the environment to protect those who are at risk. Sanford (1972) probably takes the most proactive stance on violence prevention. He notes that violence is almost always demeaning and argues that it is not enough to prevent this dehumanization and destructiveness. Rather, institutions of higher education must work to humanize and to develop constructive relationships among people. The lack of available research that concentrates specifically on the perpetrator is evident, thus providing the stimulus for this discussion. Understanding and preventing campus violence are two different things.

Clearly, all the data that exist, both reported and suspected, lead one to understand that if we are to be successful in eradicating the severity of violence on our campuses, we must also take a critical look at improving the campus culture. This includes educational initiatives that focus on the perpetrator as well (Davis, 1998). The greater challenge is to acknowledge distinctive subgroups, while attending to the general population. The institution needs to consider alternative ways of providing educational opportunity and experience, thus creating a campus of care. We also need to relinquish out-moded or narrowly conceived practices.

An increasing interest in, and commitment to, assessment of college student learning and development demands the examination of students' experiences while they are with us (Schuh & Upcraft, 2000; Upcraft & Schuh, 1996). Campus climate assessments reflect the real needs and experiences that exist among our stakeholders and can assist with making necessary improvements in the quality of campus life (Barr & Associates, 1990, 1993; Schuh & Upcraft, 2000). Assessment of campus culture through its climate should take place on a regular basis, preferably at the beginning, middle, and end of each academic year. This should not be difficult or expensive, now that we have all this technology at our fingertips. Not only is individual assessment important, but each campus should be analyzed from a systems perspective. In fact, the entire enterprise of American higher education must be looked at on a periodic and ongoing basis. A good assessment design provides indications that are necessary to address the concerns of the academy as they relate to race, gender, and sexual orientation. It will also guide efforts that support the provision of a climate that is supportive for learning, personal growth, and professional development. Not only will we need to determine what types of assessment institutions need to focus on in the future, we must realize that assessment is but one step toward civility on our campuses. Fundamental to this process is the analysis and dissemination of this information so that the appropriate action can be taken (Smith, 2001, 2011). Action indicates movement.

For our purposes, Schön's classic work on learning, reflection, and change (1967, 1983, 1991) combined with Argyris's contribution on double-loop learning that involves questioning the role of the framing and learning systems that underlie actual goals and strategies, provides the perfect theoretical context for understanding how this action affects an organization's norms, policies, and objectives (Argyris & Schön, 1974, 1978; Barr & Associates, 1988). Three elements of their theory of action that are important to this work are *governing variables*, those dimensions that people are trying to keep within acceptable limits; *action strategies*, moves and plans used by people to keep their governing values within the acceptable range; and *consequences*, what happens as a result of an action, both intended and unintended. Other classical theorists have contributed to this theory of developing critical, self-reflecting practice, and they set the framework for the following template (Dewey, 1910; Eisner, 1998; Etzioni, 1968; Hainer, 1968; Husén, 1974; Hutchins, 1970). Educational intervention is an intentional design that specifically targets both the perpetrator and the organization as they use reflection and reflective practice as a means toward understanding oneself and provides an institutional strategy for eradicating campus violence, thus creating a more comfortable learning environment. The remainder of this chapter focuses on a blueprint of an educational intervention that addresses the behavior that by intent, action, or outcome harms another person. It contains three essential elements that can be emphasized differentially in terms of interventions, namely, intent addressed through education, actions through judicial processes, and outcomes through counseling and other services (Roark, 1994a, 1994b). The proposed template addresses each of these elements.

A Concept, Philosophy, and Theory for Educational Intervention (EI)

For our purposes, campus violence and intolerant behavior are discussed as acts toward or against an individual or group of individuals as defined earlier. Conceptually we must first understand that any category of persons can become a target of violence and intolerance, although some are more predisposed than others. Additionally, we cannot be expected to control every aspect of campus life. The very nature of the college campus, its community, and the naïveté of our student population contribute to victimization because of the open, trusting, and free nature of our college campus and its community. For example, although we want our campuses to be safe, problems of safety and security are tied to lighting, shrubbery-covered walkways, evening classes, and campus events. Victimization can also result from the behavioral and psychological problems that our students bring with them. Compound these problems with the flagrant use of alcohol and drugs, and one can see how opportunities for violence are created.

Understanding the educational and developmental objective of any intervention process is extremely important. Rooted in the very heart of the curriculum, the following intervention is based on an understanding of the path of the student experience from an educational perspective. As described in Figure 5.1, learning takes place both inside and outside the formal classroom. We contend that the greater part of the student's development takes place outside the formal classroom; therefore, our model concentrates on the informal path of a student's experience. As illustrated, students come to us with a set of preconditions. Once these conditions are conjoined with any combination of other variables, such as the hidden curriculum, peer culture, or individual life experience, the individual student is faced with a variety of choices. If these choices involve the use of violence, the institution has a right and responsibility to respond.

Every student who commits and is found guilty of an act of violence will not benefit from interventions; therefore, the decision to accept a case for

Figure 5.1 The Curriculum Model

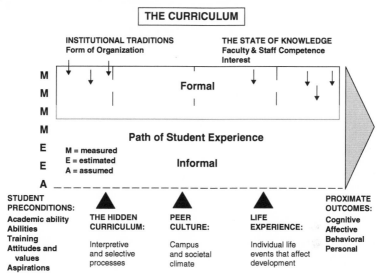

Note. Figure from a lecture for a graduate seminar on curriculum development in higher education (HEA 616, History of Higher Education, SUNY–Buffalo State). Copyright 1996, 2012 by Wanda M. Davis.

referral to educational intervention must be made by a professional on a case-by-case basis. After examining the intent of the student's behavior, only those who show promise and a willingness to participate in the intervention should be invited to take part. All others will need to go through the normal student judicial process, which usually results in expulsion. By formal contract, it is also understood that failure to successfully complete the EI could result in the student's return to the campus judicial process.

A Statement of Goals

Used as an educational alternative to, or in combination with, the traditional disciplinary process, the educational intervention acts as a supplemental sanction for documented acts of violence and intolerance. Administered through the student conduct judiciary and managed by professional staff, the goals of educational intervention initiatives are to make more hospitable the climate and learning environment on the campus, to create an educational intervention for violent behavior, to expand disciplinary sanctions to include educational experiences, to create a partnership with members of the campus community in support of educational intervention, and to build a comprehensive response to violence that includes persons from different sectors of the campus. Perhaps most significantly, the goal is to provide an experience and atmosphere where students explore differences in attitudes, values, beliefs, and appropriate ways of responding to their own anger.

One must understand that educational interventions are not intended to coerce, indoctrinate, or force a change in the attitude of those involved. Rather, by design, the intervention will expose the perpetrator to new materials, information, knowledge, and points of view. Through this structured exercise, the student is permitted to compare previously learned attitudes, beliefs, and behavior with other standards of thinking and behavior. As a direct result of the exposure, the violator's attitudes, beliefs, and behavior may change.

Program and Educational Objectives

Although expected outcomes may vary for each participant, at minimum, a number of major objectives can be identified. Those who participate will be afforded the opportunity to examine the similarities that enhance and differences that impede communication across cultural boundaries. Students involved will examine their beliefs, attitudes, and values and explore how they contribute to violent, ethnocentric, homophobic, racist, sexist, or other prejudicial behaviors. Participants will also examine their role in perpetuating or eradicating social inequality. Through a formal contract between student, mentor, and the institution, a learning environment is created where students can develop more effective communication skills. Using successful anger management strategies, they will also be required to devise a strategy for more effective interaction, particularly where violence or intolerance is evident. At minimum, the institution is providing a systematic response that includes educational intervention for those who exhibit this brutal and inappropriate behavior. Through educational interventions, the institution's commitment to promote an environment free of violence and intolerance will be evident because the guilty individual is treated at the cognitive level. Objectives of this learning process are made apparent in Figure 5.2.

Simply put, the educational objectives involve three levels of development. First, the *cognitive area* refers to the acquiring of knowledge. When students are exposed to new or different material, we expect they will come to know more. Second and third, given this additional knowledge, we hope that their *affective development* will help them to think before they act, to feel better about themselves and their contribution to society, and that active participation in their own learning will help them to adjust their *behavior* and begin to act as civilized, respectable citizens. At least we have safely addressed the issue of one's own violent behavior and the climate of the organization. Some students are beyond our help, and because the academy is about education

Figure 5.2 Student Development and Educational Objectives

Note. Figure from a lecture for a graduate seminar on curriculum development in higher education (HEA 616, History of Higher Education, SUNY–Buffalo State). Copyright 1996, 2012 by Wanda M. Davis. Adapted with permission.

rather than rehabilitation, not everyone will benefit from the experience. But, at least the academy has taken thoughtful steps to address a problem at its core as opposed to administering a quick fix to control how the institution is perceived in the public. A by-product of this thoughtful approach is that it helps to open the minds of individuals to understand why they hurt themselves or others. Of course the process has to be closely monitored, with a protocol for minimal standards for implementation.

Administration of the Program

Imperative to the success of this initiative is a clear designation of responsibility for the following major program areas: management and administration of the overall program, coordination of the educational intervention process, selection and training of mentors, and maintenance of a resource library. Management of the overall program should be entrusted to an office that has responsibility for overseeing or enforcing the student code of conduct. Placing the initiative congruent with other rules, regulations, and policies that govern student behavior provides an excellent point of institutional response to campus violence and intolerance. Second, educational interventions should be administered through a program coordinator. Cases referred from the student conduct office for educational initiative will then be carefully monitored. Selection, training, and participation of mentors is one of the most important components of the model. In a successful program the educational intervention coordinator will be largely responsible for this area. A third and very important element of the intervention is that of the trained mentor. Central to a successful mentoring relationship is the concept of self-directed learning. Through this process, with the mentor's assistance, participants remain in control of their learning. This guided learning approach makes possible the transfer of attitudes, behaviors, and skills (Davis, 1998; Sandeen & Barr, 2006).

Selecting and Training the Mentor

As a response to violent/intolerant behavior and a proven violation of the student behavior code, an agreement is reached between the judicial office and the student. Next, a formal mentoring relationship is arranged between the student and the mentor. This relationship is based on the student's need to complete an educational intervention. The relationship among the student, mentor, and judicial office must be built around the completion of an approved and agreed-upon project or activity that is articulate and signed via a written contract. Even if there are only two or three meetings between mentor and student, the educational intervention process will take time, effort, and commitment from both the student and the mentor. Consequently, the mentor needs to be carefully selected and trained so that valuable time is not spent unnecessarily. It is equally important that EI mentors be chosen from both administrative and faculty pools.

Selection begins with involvement from the president, provost, dean, or department chair and should cross ethnic, gender, religious, and sexual orientation lines. It is further recommended that mentors be chosen from outside the student affairs profession. This adds credibility, depth, and breadth to the educational process. Developing a pool of well-trained mentors who are committed to educational intervention will strengthen the opportunity for growth and development of the individual student. It will also provide the institution with a positive means for responding to campus violence. A successful intervention will attract others who might be nominated as mentors as well as engage the entire community in a collaborative effort to make the campus safer and less threatening. In the end, the campus environment will be improved for all.

Drawing upon the complex theories of self-development and self-directed learning (Strange & Banning, 2000), mentoring is a vital component to an educational process. Through mentoring, a learning environment can be created. It is important to understand that not all students who engage in violent or intolerant behavior will be afforded this opportunity. This decision for a student to participate begins with the judicial office and must be agreed to by the student. If the contract agreement is not upheld satisfactorily, the student runs the risk of going back through the traditional judicial system and being suspended from the university. The following section explains the process in more detail.

The Process of Implementation

Once a student has been identified as being in violation of a conduct code, along with having exhibited violent or intolerant behavior, the case is evaluated for possible assignment to an educational intervention. The assignment is then registered with the conduct office, and an evaluation or intake is performed by the program coordinator. The coordinator contacts a mentor to discuss an educational experience tailored to the special needs of the student, consistent with the severity of the infraction. This sequence of meetings needs to be double-checked by the coordinator. After meeting with the coordinator, the student meets with the mentor.

Within the first two meetings and a specified period of time, the student and mentor tailor the contract. The resource center library discussed in the next section will be beneficial at this stage. Because the contract is signed by both parties, the student becomes central to his or her own learning. It is the student's responsibility to obtain the correct signatures at both the beginning and end of the contract. The mentor can meet, talk with, or visit with the student or coordinator as needed. However, the intervention must be completed within a period specified but no longer than two semesters in the initial contract. The coordinator conducts the final follow-up session with the student. Questions about the process lie with the coordinator, whereas final disposition is the responsibility of the judicial office.

Resource Center Library

A collection of readings, videos, games, equipment, and other educational materials/tools is made available for use through the resource center library. The use of technology and social networks is also very helpful. Resources to be collected and maintained will be important to the design and ultimate effectiveness of the intervention. The tools should reflect the goals and objectives of the tailored assignment. That is, they should provide offenders with an opportunity to examine their values and beliefs, their verbal and nonverbal language, and their activities as they relate to violent and intolerant behavior. Supplementing the holdings of the library with campus activities or involvement in program implementation is also suggested.

In the beginning, the resource center should address at minimum the issues of violence, focusing on intercultural communication, sexual orientation, and women. Subcategories, such as alcohol, drugs, and abusive relationships, could be the next grouping. Once established, the center holdings should grow to reflect the nature of violence that exists on the individual campus. The success of the intervention for the participant, the program, and the institution will be uninterrupted. As with any library, this one will need a key person to monitor, distribute, and purchase materials. A tripartite steering committee consisting of faculty, staff, and students can assess the quality and effective use of library holdings. It is recommended that materials be categorized by type as they relate to violence. It is equally important to understand that this intervention is aimed at prevention, and the experience is geared toward working with perpetrators as they examine their role in either fostering or eradicating social injustice. Through this structured agreement students plainly develop and devise a strategy for more effective and appropriate behavior.

Program Assessment

As stated, the intent of this educational intervention is not to *brainwash* or manipulate attitudes but to require student exposure to new information, knowledge, and points of view. After this experience, students should be able to compare their previously learned values, attitudes, and behaviors with a new and different set of ethics for thinking and acting. Attitudinal change often occurs over time, and therefore, attitudes and values may not be completely apparent at the end of the intervention. However, the quality of the experience should inhibit negative behavior. Referral to personal evaluation and focus groups can further help to assess individual growth and development. Assessment can also be based on feedback from mentors. As with focus groups, identification of problems, concerns, and success will be followed up with action by the coordinator. Direct response from students is also important. Remember, the process is as important as what students consciously learn from the experience. Although concrete learning may come later, violators will learn to manage their approach toward handling violence and intolerance in a more interpersonally effective and socially civil manner.

Through this process, mentors will have increased confidence in themselves and the very important role they have in changing an institution's culture. As the institution realizes that it can make a difference in students' lives and that it can effectively combat campus violence and intolerance, this approach can be successfully incorporated on any campus. The design and copyright are registered with the Library of Congress through the United States Copyright Office, with the author having copyright claims.[1]

Conclusion

As we move into the future, the American college system will need to understand the lessons learned from institutions that have created positive learning experiences on their campuses. This is extremely important, because results can be instructive as we move to educate our various constituents and subsets within the organization. Educational intervention is a proactive response that interrupts the cycle of violence by addressing the disruptive behavior of perpetrators, by ensuring that they understand their responsibility to the community. This intervention is one response that can be used to address violence on our college campuses. It is designed as a selective program geared toward working with those who show a readiness to grow and to learn about respecting themselves and others. At minimum, the response begins with assessment, intervention, more assessment, and evaluation.

Failure to assess individual campuses and higher education as a whole will undoubtedly leave America at a loss. If we do not understand the complexity of higher education and how diversity affects decisions within the system as a whole, we are doomed to continue to provide educational environments that fall prey to civil animosity, misunderstanding, and suspicion. This is not to say that there has been no progress toward achieving diversity; however, this chapter is written with the understanding that on the whole American higher education has yet to handle the perpetrators of campus violence. This responsibility lies with the game changers in the academy.

Note

1. "An Educational Model for Sanctioning Acts Motivated by Intolerance." Copyright 1991 by Wanda M. Davis, registration number TXu000496021. The public catalog copyright record is available from http://cocatalog.loc.gov.

References

Almedia, D. A. (1993). Introduction to campus tensions in Massachusetts. *Equity and Excellence in Education, 26*(1), 6–8.

Argyris, C., & Schön, D. (1974). *Theory in practice: Increasing professional effectiveness.* San Francisco, CA: Jossey-Bass.

Argyris, C., & Schön, D. (1978). *Organizational learning: A theory of action perspective.* San Francisco, CA: Jossey-Bass.

Banyard, V. L., Moynihan, M. M., & Crossman, M. T. (2009). Reducing sexual violence on campus: The role of student leaders as empowered bystanders. *Journal of College Student Development, 50*(4), 446–457.

Barr, M. J., & Associates. (1988). *Student services and the law: A handbook for practitioners.* San Francisco, CA: Jossey-Bass.

Barr, M. J., & Associates. (1990). *New futures for student affairs*. San Francisco, CA: Jossey-Bass.

Barr, M. J., & Associates. (1993). *Student affairs administration*. San Francisco, CA: Jossey-Bass.

Bromley, M. L. (2005). *Campus-related murders: A content analysis review of news articles*. Paper presented at the Annual Conference of the Southern Criminal Justice Association. Retrieved September 25, 2008, from http://www.dcf.state.fl.us. Updated link retrieved on April 14, 2010, from http://www.dcf.state.fl.us/initiatives/campussecurity/docs/Campus_Related_Murders050907.pdf

Cantalupo, N. C. (2009). Campus violence: Understanding the extraordinary through the ordinary. *Journal of College and University Law, 35,* 613–690.

Davis, W. (1996). Educational intervention: A prescription for violence prevention at historically black colleges and universities. *Journal of Negro Education, 65*(4), 454–461.

Davis, W. (1998). Toward civility: Assessment as a means toward improving campus climate. *College Student Affairs Journal, 18*(1), 72–84.

Davis, W. (2012, September 11). Presentation, National ASALH Conference, Richmond, VA.

Davis, W. M., & Dulski, C. (2001). Give peace a chance: College students protest and the Civil Rights Movement, 1960–1975. *American Educational History Journal, 28,* 55–59.

Davis, W., & Richbart, C. A. (1998). A simmering controversy: African American students and diversity at predominantly white campuses. *National Association of Student Affairs Professionals, 1*(1), 85–92.

Dewey, J. (1910). *How we think.* New York: D. C. Heath.

Drysdale, D. A., Modzeleski, W., & Simons, A. (2010). *Campus attacks: Targeted violence affecting institutions of higher education*. Washington, DC: U.S. Secret Service, U.S. Department of Homeland Security; Office of Safe and Drug-Free Schools, U.S. Department of Education; Federal Bureau of Investigation, U.S. Department of Justice.

Eisner, E. W. (1998). *The enlightened eye: Qualitative inquiry and the enhancement of educational practice.* Upper Saddle River, NJ: Prentice Hall.

Etzioni, A. (1968). *The active society: The theory of societal and political processes.* New York: Free Press.

Family Educational Rights and Privacy Act, 34 U.S.C. § 99. Appendix A, crimes of violence definitions. (1974).

Hainer, R. M. (1968). Rationalism, pragmatism and existentialism. In E. Glatt & M. W. Shelly (Eds.), *The research society.* New York: Gordon and Breach.

Hayes, D. W. (1993). Campus violence upsurge forces legislation, student initiatives. *Black Issues in Higher Education, 10,* 20–22.

Hayes, D. W. (1994). Violence: Another burden for some HBCUs. *Black Issues in Higher Education, 10,* 22–25.

Hemphill, B., Roberts, G., & LaBanc, B. (2010). *Enough is enough: A student affairs perspective on preparedness and response to a campus shooting.* Sterling, VA: Stylus.

Husén, T. (1974). *The learning society.* London: Methuen.

Hutchins, R. M. (1970). *The learning society.* London: Penguin.

Hutchinson, E. O. (2007, April 17). Massacre exposes America's campus violence. *The Albion Monitor.* Retrieved from http://www.monitor.net/monitor/0704a/ copyright/virginiatechcampusguns.html

Langford, L. (2004). *Preventing violence and promoting safety in higher education settings: Overview of a comprehensive approach.* Washington, DC: The U.S. Department of Education's Higher Education Center for Alcohol, Drug Abuse, and Violence Prevention.

Lederman, D. (1994). A tragic toll. *The Chronicle of Higher Education, 41,* A35–A36.

Lederman, D. (1995). Colleges report rise in violent crime. *The Chronicle of Higher Education, 41*(21), A41–A42.

Meggett, L. L. (1994). Unfinished business. *Black Issues in Higher Education, 11,* 24–26.

Nicoletti, J., Spencer-Thomas, S., & Bollinger, C. (2001). *Violence goes to college: The authoritative guide to prevention and intervention.* Springfield, IL: Charles C. Thomas.

Office of Postsecondary Education. (2008). http://ope.ed.gov/security/Group Details.aspx

O'Neil, R. M. (1989, October 18). Colleges should seek educational alternatives to rules that override the historic guarantees of free speech. *The Chronicle of Higher Education,* B1, B3.

Orzek, A. M. (1989). *Campus violence and campus discrimination.* St. Louis, MO: American College Personnel Association.

Palmer, C. J. (1993). *Violent crimes and other forms of victimization in residence halls.* Asheville, NC: College Administration Publications.

Paludi, M. A. (Ed.). (2008). *Understanding and preventing campus violence.* Westport, CT: Praeger.

Potter, S. J., Moynihan, M. M., & Stapleton, J. G. (2011). Using social self-identification in social marketing materials aimed at reducing violence against women on campus. *Journal of Interpersonal Violence, 26*(5), 971–990.

Reynolds, A. (1989, June). *Hiding from each other? Sexuality in a diverse community.* ACPA Developments. St. Louis, MO: American College Personnel Association.

Reynolds, A., Lustgraaf, M., & Bogar, C. (1989, January). *Institutional response to campus violence.* ACPA Developments, 4, pp. 58–59. St. Louis, MO: American College Personnel Association.

Reynolds, A. L., & Von Destinon, M. (Eds.). (1993). *Campus violence manual.* St. Louis, MO: American College Personnel Association.

Reynolds, A., Roark, M., Shang, P., & Stevens, M. (1988, November). *Incidents of campus violence.* ACPA Developments, 7.

Roark, M. L. (1987). Preventing violence on college campuses. *Journal of Counseling and Development, 65*(7), 367–371.

Roark, M. L. (1988). *Guide for preventing campus violence.* St. Louis, MO: American College Personnel Association.

Roark, M. L. (1990, April). *Nevitt Sanford on violence. From: The ethics of campus violence interventions: Going beyond prevention.* Paper presented at a meeting of the American College Personnel Association, St. Louis, MO.

Roark, M. L. (1994a). Back to basics on campus violence prevention: The multicultural campus violence intervention model. *College Student Personnel Association Journal, 1993–1994, 35–38.*

Roark, M. L. (1994b). Conceptualizing campus violence: Definitions, underlying factors and effects. *Journal of College Student Psychotherapy, 8*(1/2), 1–28.

Sandeen, A., & Barr, M. (2006). *Critical issues for student affairs.* San Francisco, CA: Jossey-Bass.

Sanford, N. (1972). Collective destructiveness: Sources and remedies. In G. Used (Ed.), *Perspectives on* violence (pp. 33–87). New York: Brunner/Mazel.

Schön, D. A. (1967). *Technology and change: The new Heraclitus.* Oxford: Pergamon Press.

Schön, D. A. (1983). The reflective practitioner: How professionals think in action. London: Temple Smith.

Schön, D. A. (1991). *The reflective turn: Case studies in and on educational practice.* New York: Teachers Press, Columbia University.

Schuh, J., & Upcraft, M. (2000). *Assessment practice in student affairs.* San Francisco, CA: Jossey-Bass.

Scribner, R., Mason, K., Simonsen, N. R., Theal, K., Chotalia, J., Johnson, S. I., . . . DeJong, W. (2010). An ecological analysis of alcohol-outlet density and campus-reported violence at 32 U.S. colleges. *Journal of Studies on Alcohol and Drugs, 71*(12), 184–191.

Shang, P., & Stevens, M. (1988). *Standing committee on campus violence. ACPA Developments, 3,* St. Louis, MO: American College Personnel Association.

Smith, M. K. (2001, 2011). Schön: Learning, reflection and change, *The encyclopedia of informal education.* Retrieved from www.infed.org/thinkers/et-schon.htm

Snow, B. A., & Thro, W. E. (1994). Redefining the contours of university liability: The potential implications of Nero v. Kansas State University. *West's Educational Law Journal, 3*(4), 541–557.

Stith, S. M., Jester, S. B., & Bird, G. W. (1992). A typology of college students who use violence in their dating relationships. *Journal of College Student Development, 33,* 411–421.

Strange, C., & Banning, J. (2000). *Educating by design: Creating campus learning environments that work.* San Francisco, CA: Jossey-Bass.

Upcraft, M., & Schuh, J. (1996). *Assessment in student affairs: A guide for practitioners.* San Francisco, CA: Jossey-Bass.

6

DIALOGUE, REFLECTION, AND LEARNING

From Our (Spiritual) Center

Richanne C. Mankey

"Teaching students to engage in reflective thinking and to make reflective judgments about vexing problems is a central goal of higher education."

—*King & Kitchener, 1994, p. 222*

The best way to meet the goal King and Kitchener purport is for us to model a reflective practice in our daily professional life for students. Effective student affairs professionals meet students where they are in order to assist them to move from their dependence on home to an independent life after graduation from college. To inspire their engagement with reflection for learning, it is useful to consciously incorporate our own reflection into the equation. Knowing where we are is an important component if we are to *meet students where they are* without invoking our values on them.

My career focus has been, either formally or informally, consciously or subconsciously, on facilitating learning in myself and others. Central to learning with others is dialogue that assists students to clarify and live their own values. Dialogue is pivotal to challenging and supporting students outside of the classroom. Although this chapter focuses specifically on traditionally aged college students, the practices and ways of being I put forth are important for all human interactions among students, faculty, colleagues, family members, and friends.

Many authors' wisdom on one's lifelong journey has facilitated my own reflection on my values, their origins, my biases, my weaknesses, and my strengths, which have given me insight into my administrative style, my effectiveness with students, and my ability to stay centered in difficult situations. It is a continually imperfect process of reflection in action that helps me engage with others as authentically as possible. Schön (1983) said, "Reflection is an 'art' by which practitioners sometimes deal well with situations of uncertainty, instability, uniqueness, and value conflict" (p. 50). To me, reflection serves us best when we look inward to our own intentions, emotions, and actions in order to compare them with what we espouse our beliefs to be. Unfortunately, sometimes what we discover is dissonant and therefore unpleasant to acknowledge. I contend that we reflect anyway. Reflection is not, however, a path to perfection; I have come to believe that perfection in our human form is not possible. The journey of continual alignment and realignment of our espoused beliefs with our behavior is important to our continued growth and integrity. Students will not believe us if we say, for instance, we believe in respectful behavior when they experience us acting disrespectfully.

When we use reflection to discern our own place in life, we are better able to engage in a meaningful dialogue with students. My practice as a senior student affairs officer (SSAO) is grounded in Perry's scheme (1968/1999) as the basis for understanding student development and meeting students where they are. The spiritual wisdom of Ruiz and Ruiz's (2010) five agreements has enabled me to reflect on my own practice of meeting students where they are. I assert that Ruiz's agreements combined with Mezirow's transformative learning theory (1990, 2000, 2003) help us first to understand our own beliefs and dilemmas. And I assert these theories may help us facilitate difficult conversations with students and colleagues in a less judgmental, and therefore, more effective way. In this chapter, I use Ruiz and Ruiz's and Mezirow's theories to suggest practical methods for discerning our own beliefs, facilitating reflection through dialogue, and creating a learning environment of *mutual* care and compassion. I offer an example from my own practice as a reference point for our "dialogue." On my own journey, I have found that authentic dialogue with students facilitates their gleaning the most from their out-of-the-classroom learning.

Meeting Students Where They Are: Engaging Reflection and Dialogue

Often faculty members lament, "Students these days are not prepared for college." My response is, "They are where they are." Perhaps they are not where we would like them to be, yet students' admission was granted based on acceptable and agreed-upon criteria. Consequently, it becomes our responsibility to acknowledge where students are, trusting that the potential for college success indicated by their admission can be realized. Student affairs professionals are central to facilitating the realization of students' potential. It is my responsibility to remind faculty that perhaps students are not where we would like them to be academically or socially. Yet, if we can suspend our judging lens of "woulda, shoulda, coulda" and can instead discern their level of development, students are more likely to both learn and mature.

Perry's scheme (1968/1999) helps us discern where students are. His work is most valuable when used as a reminder that students are on a continuum of development—no matter what we think about where they (or their parents) should be. At the beginning of the development continuum is dualism (right-and-wrong thinking); on the other end is commitment to relativism (ability to make commitments amid the ambiguity of life). Our role is to challenge and support students on their journey to relativism and independence.

A small but frequent example of a way we might challenge and support is e-mail. I have come to embrace the opportunity to use my "favorite" e-mail greeting from a student as a way to encourage professional communication. I want to help students see that "hey" is not an appropriate greeting for me as the SSAO, for a faculty advisor, or for a supervisor at his or her first professional position. My response is typically:

> Dear [name (or username as such e-mail is not typically signed)]: Thank you for your inquiry about [insert topic]. I am forwarding your message to [staff member] for response. As you continue your education, I encourage you to consider that a greeting of "hey" is inappropriate for professional use. It is more appropriate to use a formal greeting, such as "Dear Dean Mankey." It is also appropriate to use a formal closing, such as "Sincerely yours, [your name]" along with contact information so you can be reached directly. Thank you, Dean Mankey

After almost two decades of Millennial students (born between approximately 1978 and 2000) (Howe & Strauss, 2000) and their "helicopter" parents, my assertion is that students have been *protected, provided for,* but not necessarily *parented* in a way that promotes their independence. I call these the three *Ps* (3Ps). My designation of the 3Ps grew from my own experience and increasingly more frequent comments from faculty and staff members about students' seeming inability and, more disturbingly, unwillingness to seek needed services or resolution to their campus concerns. These observations were coupled with an increased frequency of parental contact with campus personnel to resolve student issues *for* their students. When I would express these 3Ps to those articulating their concerns, the concept of "protected provided for, and not necessarily parented" resonated with them. The 3Ps provided a sensitivity that made it easier for me to meet everyone on campus—including students' parents—where they are.

To meet them where they are in order to challenge and support them to independence, students benefit from our support, encouragement, and discernment as well as firm, direct, and compassionate confrontation of issues; our judgment is a deterrent to learning. One important way to offer these values to students is by developing or enhancing our own practice of reflection. When we are centered and meeting students authentically, we are better able to effectively address issues of concern, and they are better able to respond to those issues of concern to them. Thus, they are able to perceive and feel they are not being judged; only held accountable for inappropriate actions. By holding them accountable both inside and outside the classroom for learning—academically, socially, emotionally, spiritually—we aid their success after they have secured a degree.

To illustrate, the story in Box 6.1 is from a real conduct issue. As part of the disciplinary process, it is important to reflect about our interactions with students and learn from them. As we began to prepare to deal with this complaint, a staff member and I actually reflected before the disciplinary meeting with the student. We pulled his file and refamiliarized ourselves with his documented behavior. Unfortunately, we saw a pattern to his behavior that seemed likely to culminate in an increased chance he would act out and hurt someone, not just a wall or a chair. Although our prior actions were appropriate, we saw a need to address the pattern of his behavior that seemed to follow a cycle of violence (see Figure 6.1). We addressed his pattern, not by pointing it out to him at the beginning of the disciplinary meeting, but by listening to him. *After* we listened to him, we shared our observations and why they were of concern to us. We went beyond the hard, fast rules and addressed the person. Our goal was not just the acute situation of his and others' safety, but, equally as important, his ability to function productively and without violence as an adult with a bachelor's degree.

Box 6.1

Recently I worked with a student who had parted ways with a girlfriend. She complained that he wouldn't leave her alone and was "keeping track" of her by watching her and sending endless text messages. She feared his tendency to get violent when consuming alcohol. In conversation with the young man, he admitted his "obsession" with the young woman and said it wouldn't happen again. His file, however, revealed a similar incident in the past, so we talked about an emerging pattern of behavior that could be destructive to him, her, and his college career. In the prior situation, disciplinary action had been taken and counseling required. The young man had satisfied his requirements, yet it now was apparent that learning had not occurred. He was close to graduation, and his academic career teetered on the edge of his behavior. I took a chance. I met him at the heart level and verbalized my observations about him, his behavior, recurring patterns, and my suspicions about what might be behind all of this. He broke down and told me of a volatile home life, his parents' divorce, and that he faced living and working in the same community as his parent who expressed emotions through violence. Aha! I talked to him about a basic "cycle of violence" to let him know why I believed he was sorry for his behavior yet didn't believe his current apology would hold water when a difficult situation arose in the future. The diagram in Figure 6.1 helped me show him that he was now in the "honeymoon" stage and truly was sorry, and that there would most likely be a shift, soon, to "tension building," which would most likely lead to an "explosion." I explained that if an individual can begin to intervene in the tension-building stage, a destructive explosion can often be avoided. And I indicated that it is not easy work. At the end of my explanation, he looked me in the eye and said that he was ready to admit he saw this cycle in himself. He said he had been too "scared" to admit it and he didn't want to be like his parents. Now the learning could begin, because he was willing to take an honest look inside himself.

Figure 6.1 Cycle of Violence

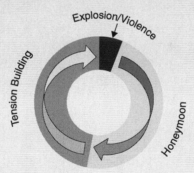

Note. Adapted from Coalition Against Violence–Avalon East (n.d.).

As I reflected on the situation in Box 6.1, I knew the student should have been suspended. He would not have graduated and would have left with his violent tendencies ineffectively addressed. We were willing to take a risk and support him in finding more acceptable ways than violence to address his stressors (see Box 6.2). I realize he is not the only student who has not progressed to a commitment to relativism by graduation. Additionally, just because someone is chronologically beyond college age does not necessarily mean he or she has progressed beyond dualism. Thus, it is important to meet students—all people—where they are. Yet the question begs: Just how do we develop a reflective practice?

Box 6.2

The student who became ready to admit his issues worked hard on his violent tendencies and graduated on time. Shortly after graduation, he returned to campus to attend an event. As I walked through the student center, he approached me, asked if he could give me a hug, and thanked me for calling him on his issues. He continues the difficult work of reflecting, being self-aware in difficult situations, and becoming the person he chooses to be—an intelligent, fun-loving, generous man who now respects others' boundaries and his own wishes to be free of violence.

Reflection and Dialogue: Using the Five Agreements

My personal reflective practice was advanced by ancient Toltec wisdom. The five agreements (Ruiz, 1997; Ruiz & Ruiz, 2010) give us a practical structure through which to launch our own personal and spiritual growth using reflection. The structure is simple, yet the work is intense, ongoing, and transformational. It is not easy to practice the ongoing spiritual dialogue with ourselves that Ruiz and Ruiz (2010) suggest. When we choose to do the personal work, transformative learning is promoted in ourselves, thus in others.

It is concerning that we have been domesticated to look to others to change and that much of our public dialogue and our legal system is structured to promote this view (Ruiz & Ruiz, 2010). As I continue to grow and develop, one of the most significant realizations I have had is that when I change myself others may change in response to my changes. What I know (and often forget acutely) is that I have absolutely no control over others' behavior; I can *only* inspire them to think and act differently. I spent the better part of my life and career using precious personal energy to wish things were different. I call it my "if only" syndrome—a syndrome I set out to change *in myself.* Meeting ourselves where we are and realizing that what we can control lies within us is directly and immediately applicable to our work with students.

Learning to promote self-development in ourselves and others is multidimensional work. It is spiritual, cognitive, emotional, and physical. In developing a practice of reflection, Ruiz and Ruiz's (2010) work focuses on spiritual development. To truly benefit from ancient wisdom, I learned to suspend my twenty-first-century lens to understand that our current view of the world is only one way of knowing; ancient civilizations used their own tools to discern the universe, too. Interestingly enough, some of their calculations have proven true. For instance, more than 2,000 years ago the Maya, an indigenous culture related to the Toltec, predicted that the first cell of life appeared about 1.5 billion years ago; in the late 1990s scientists discovered with a supercomputer that the first cell appeared about 1.5 billion years ago. The former used astronomy and base-20 manual mathematical calculations; the latter used a twentieth-century supercomputer. The lesson is that knowledge and wisdom come in many forms if we use all available tools effectively in our lifetime. Toltec wisdom offers five agreements:

1. Be impeccable with your word,
2. Don't take anything personally,
3. Don't make assumptions,
4. Always do your best, and
5. Be skeptical but learn to listen.

The five agreements are summarized in what follows. Ruiz and Ruiz (2010) frame them within a larger context of how we each have been domesticated to see the world through the lens of our own cultural upbringing, religious teachings, country of origin, socioeconomic influences, and social mores.

The First Agreement: Be impeccable with your word. The wisdom of this agreement is to say what is authentic to us and what we know to be true. Gossip, for instance, is something we know is most likely false; thus, the agreement encourages us not to engage in gossip. It also advises us to say what we mean as plainly (and lovingly) as possible and not to say what we think someone else needs us to say. Thus, it challenges us to discover and say what is true to us. The first agreement is foundational to all the other agreements.

The Second Agreement: Don't take anything personally. So many concerns in our life arise when we take things personally. Following the wisdom of the second agreement, when we are offended because we think something is directed at us, it is an assumption. Many things affect other people in human interactions that may have nothing to do with us and everything to do with them. When we assume that what happened was directed toward us, we are taking things personally.

The Third Agreement: Don't make assumptions. When we make assumptions, this agreement reminds us, we base our thinking and speaking on information that may not be true. Our assumption is only a perception from our own lens and our own biases—it has nothing to do with the intention or motivation of the "other"; it has everything to do with what we think we know. The wisdom of this agreement encourages us to ask when we suspect we know the opinion or motivation of someone else. It also advises us that making judgments inhibits the use of our energy for good, whereas discerning our own feelings and thoughts about a matter is imperative.

The Fourth Agreement: Always do your best. This agreement advises us to do our best—in life and in practicing the agreements—in order not to judge ourselves. Toltec wisdom says that we should only give 100 percent of our energy to whatever we are doing, not ever more than 100 percent, because then we deplete our own energy and have nothing left to give to ourselves or others. And it helps us to stay in the present and can eliminate our human tendency to self-deprecate. When we think *do our best*, it reminds us to reflect in action. We may find we have not been impeccable with our words, for instance. We acknowledge it and know that we can do our best tomorrow. It is not a pass to be mediocre; rather, it is an agreement to do our best. When we do, we alleviate guilt and fear and commit to do our best—always.

The original four agreements (Ruiz, 1997) are not about creating perfection within our human existence, but instead, they are about providing a framework through which we can create awareness of our own practices and reflect upon them. The fifth agreement (Ruiz & Ruiz, 2010) underscores our human existence striving to realize the interconnectedness with all life—not just human life.

The Fifth Agreement: Be skeptical but learn to listen. At first, it seems the fifth agreement might be advising us to be skeptical of others. It is actually asking us to be skeptical of ourselves and how we have received and processed information from others. When we assign "woulda, shoulda, coulda" to someone else, we are actually giving energy to events we cannot control. In developing a practice of reflection, this agreement provides a frame to see what issues *we*, not the "other," are bringing to the situation at hand. It also encourages us to be skeptical of information and how it resonates—or not—with our values and beliefs.

In a class I teach called Transformational Leadership, we use the five agreements as a lens through which to reflect using dialogue. Students have noted in dialogue that it is easy to find tenets that we can believe in; it is more difficult to actually practice them, because we are shifting our habits of being (Yorks & Kasl, 2002). Our educational system has generally taught us to learn and regurgitate information to receive an outcome such as a grade. True learning occurs through reflection, because it helps us critically think, analyze, and feel in order to transform our life and thus the lives of those around us. Ancient Toltec wisdom reminds us: We transform others by transforming ourselves.

From the Five Agreements to Transformative Learning in Student Affairs

My personal transformation using the five agreements, I reflected, was relevant to transformative learning theory (Mezirow, 1990, 1991, 2000, 2003). *Transformative learning* is:

> [T]he process by which we transform our taken-for-granted frames of reference . . . to make them more inclusive, discriminating, open, emotionally capable of change, and reflective so that they may generate beliefs and opinions that will prove more true or justified to guide action. (Mezirow, 2000, pp. 7–8)

Mezirow (2003) advanced from a rational frame of transformative learning (Mezirow, 1990) to a metacognitive frame for such learning. Mezirow now encourages us to seek our life's purpose. Thus, he acknowledges the many ways humans learn beyond just *the rational* no matter in what ideology—or hegemony—we find ourselves. Reflection is important to transformative learning. Through it we may understand our own values and beliefs rather than living others' beliefs for us or, worse yet, living how we think they want us to live (Mezirow, 2003).

Transformative learning typically begins with a *disorienting dilemma* (Mezirow, 1990). For example, in the example in Box 6.1, the student's disorienting dilemma might be that he faced suspension from school during his senior year. We helped him identify his disorienting dilemma by approaching him from our authentic selves while staying open to him, his story, and a discussion about the situation at hand. He was then better positioned to engage in an opportunity to learn based on the disconnect *he* saw between his behavior and who he wanted to be. This powerful insight contrasts with our trying to invoke the learning and the disciplinary sanctions *on* him. Ruiz and Ruiz (2010) inspire us to transform ourselves; Mezirow (2003) inspires us to promote transformative learning in ourselves and others and suggests that as educators we can assist learners to understand why they think, feel, and believe as they do by:

1. Critically assessing the validity of their own assumptions and those of others;
2. Analyzing and assessing the source, nature and consequences of assumptions;

3. Empathizing and providing emotional support for others to engage in transformative learning;

4. Learning to participate more fully and effectively in reflective discourse to assess the reasons for a belief or perspective;

5. Anticipating the consequences of acting upon a transformed perspective and planning effective action; and

6. Developing the disposition to think critically, assess one's own assumptions, and those of others, participate fully and freely in reflective discourse, and engage in cultural or social action to improve the conditions necessary to encourage adult learners to share these insights. (p. 4)

Developing or strengthening an existing reflective practice helps us stay centered and be proactive, not reactive. Students feel more valued and have a better chance of learning if we are proactive. Conversely, a reaction may send students into a defensive mode where learning is more difficult because *winning* the argument becomes the objective, not learning.

Implications for Reflection and Dialogue

Because of my own conscious process of transformation, I realized that as an SSAO I was already promoting learning—transformative learning—in college students. And because of my awareness of power issues in research, I chose a methodology for my doctoral research that was *with* not *on* people. Accordingly my learning shifted the power dynamic in disciplinary situations from "what can I do about this behavior?" to "how will I/we promote learning for this student?"

Reflecting can take at least three physical forms: individual reflection, journal writing, and group work. In individual reflection, we each assess ourselves in an introverted manner, make mental notes for being more aware of "reflection in action" in the future, and then begin to heighten our awareness of changes we choose to make.

Individual reflection can become more valuable through journal writing. As we develop a practice of journal writing, we tend to become increasingly more comfortable revealing our own humanness. The benefit of keeping a journal over time is that we can reread our entries to see any patterns of behavior or thinking. When we see patterns, we can develop a heightened awareness of how and when our humanness is likely to manifest so we can reflect in action. "This kind of reflection in action is central to the artistry with which practitioners sometimes make new sense of uncertain, unique or conflicted situations" (Schön, 1987, p. 35).

Group reflection occurs when a trusted group, even just a pair, of people engages in dialogue to reflect and therefore raise each other's awareness of issues related to student interaction, leadership, administration, and learning.

It is important that there is trust and respect in such a relationship, as each will be sharing, challenging, and supporting personal and professional issues.

For instance, after a staff member and I meet with a student about a conduct issue, the two of us often continue to meet for a few minutes to immediately reflect about our process and our dialogue with the student. These meetings are not necessarily about the process or the student, but more about our own behavior and dialogue during the interaction. When the learning is significant or a new blind spot is revealed, I capture that learning in my journal, so that I can heighten my awareness and check myself in the future.

Because the five agreements (Ruiz, 1997; Ruiz & Ruiz, 2010) have become so important to my own development and awareness, this year my staff and I are using them to focus our work as student (people)-centered professionals. Our plan is to first methodically discuss the agreements, discern what resonates with us, and determine how we might use them in our daily work with students and colleagues. At each staff meeting, we will reflect on our use (or not) of the agreements in our work with students. Individuals may choose to keep a journal about their progress. Perhaps we are taking a risk.

F E A R of Being Authentic: Of What Are We Afraid?

"Fear creates fear, my Lords." —*Queen Elizabeth in* Elizabeth: The Golden Age. *(Kapur, 2008)*

Sometimes we are risk-averse because fear has been pervasive in our lives. We are inundated with messages of fear in advertisements; schools; working environments; and, in some cases, families. Higher education, unfortunately, is also fraught with an underlying message of fear. For example, some students are afraid to ask faculty members legitimate questions about course materials for fear of grade retaliation. There are many examples. Fear in our workplace makes us afraid to express an opinion for fear of political retaliation; it promotes communication that we assume others want to hear (Argyris & Schön, 1974).

To promote out-of-the-classroom learning and equitable application of conduct policies, we want to challenge and support students in a fear-free zone. But we do not always. Even when we have good intentions, we are often quick to judge a situation, especially a disciplinary one, by the way we *think* we see it. Valid opinions and observations from security officers and residence life staff inform our opinion. Thus, we often meet the student in question with those biases. Consequently, once we have expressed our opinion to that student, he or she may be afraid to express what happened from his or her perspective. It is likely when we talk before we listen, we create fear. Inadvertently we create fear just because our positions hold authority.

Covey (1989) provides us a perspective to help us conduct an open dialogue with a student that may be fear-free and readily promote learning from a negative situation. Covey's (1989) fifth habit is "seek first to understand, then to be understood." When we begin a disciplinary conversation by asking the student to explain what happened from his or her perspective, we open the door to dialogue. That satisfies the first half of the habit. Once we have heard from the student, we can then provide our perspective based on the appropriate guidelines and the adverse effect the behavior may have had on the community. Providing this information satisfies the second half of the habit. In this sort of dialogue, a natural tendency to be fearful or defensive is lessened and the ability to reveal issues foundational to the student's behavior is heightened. As in the example provided (Box 6.1), the dialogue provided insight into pervasive issues that were affecting the student's behavior. Due to an understanding of the cycle of violence, we were able to address deeper issues and promote the student's understanding that, although he was sorry, he would likely do it again unless he committed to some difficult personal change through reflection.

Fear can be an acronym for "False Evidence Appearing Real." It helps us understand that students may fear us and we may fear difficult interactions with students. When we pay attention to ourselves and our processes, we can move the interaction from fear (defensive) to the dialogue (productive) of transformative learning.

Averting fear and working with ourselves and students from where we are to promote the best versions of ourselves and others is ultimately an act of unconditional love. Unconditional love is giving love to another—regardless of his or her behavior—just because the person exists. It is analogous to meeting others with positive human regard. Unconditional love promotes meeting each other at the heart level and not at the level of our own expectation or from outlined policies of behavior. A frame of unconditional love allows us to use the five agreements to ask and answer these questions:

- In what ways might I look at the situation differently?
- How do I want to feel and conduct myself in this situation?
- In what ways might I choose to respond, not react? (Cook, 2009)

And, as professionals and students of higher education/student affairs administration and adult education, an honest assessment of our own behavior tells us that we do not automatically succeed when we decide to change a belief or a behavior—it is a process to actually behave using a new way of being. Whether it is a decision to eat no more chocolate or to heighten awareness to decrease our own process of making assumptions and judgments, we rarely succeed at the first pass. The five agreements, if nothing else, give us permission to be imperfect, live in the place we find ourselves, commit to our changes, and do it better the next time. They are not an excuse to behave badly or to skip the deep, personal work. They enable us to release any societal, parental, or self-invoked need to be perfect. The fourth agreement gives us permission to be perfectly imperfect.

Conclusion

Many of us choose or are in the process of choosing the profession of student affairs because we want to make a difference in the lives of students. And, once in the profession, we realize that students make a difference in *our* lives, too. We realize the mutual benefit through reflection.

Truly promoting undergraduate students' learning requires us to be aware of our own values to ensure we lead with and from our authentic self. The five agreements, if internalized and practiced, can give us a framework around which to reflect. After our interactions with students and colleagues, we may ask ourselves if we practiced the agreements to the best of our ability. Did I use my words impeccably? Did I make any assumptions, or am I still making assumptions? Did I take something someone said or did personally? Did I give my best? Did I listen with compassion for the person and skepticism of myself? As we answer these questions we can focus on our values and our interactions. The point is to be self-discerning, not self-deprecating, in order to promote our ongoing development.

While we discern our own learning, we might also ask how we are inspiring transformative learning through reflection in others (Mezirow, 1990, 2000, 2003). It is my belief that when we find ways to promote lifelong learning, we "continue the play" (Carse, 1986, p. 3). According to Carse (1986), "There are at least two kinds of games. One could be called finite, the other infinite. A finite game is played for the purpose of winning; an infinite game is played for the purpose of continuing the play" (p. 3). Occasionally, our campus colleagues are frustrated, or at least slightly skeptical, of the processes we use in student affairs. Fear not! Cone (2011) interprets Carse to say that the finite game is played for outcomes, whereas the infinite game is played through process. In higher education we value outcomes that justify our existence and answer societal criticisms of higher education and its cost. However, one of our most important outcomes, it seems, is to continue the play. Not only do we want students to persist, we want graduates to have the knowledge and skills to embark on dynamic and fulfilling professions; we also want them to have life skills conducive to productive and stimulating lives.

As we near the end of the Millennial generation of students, employers tell us, generally, that recent students, their new employees, are not prepared for professional life after college graduation. Although most graduates are found to have the correct skills to do the tasks at hand, they reportedly lack the softer skills such as communicating effectively with others, understanding that organizational politics exist and how to navigate them, using good interpersonal skills, or developing a work ethic that fits into the ethos of the organization. In student affairs we are naturally positioned to take the opportunity to address these issues in our encounters with students.

Reflection on and dialogue about our own learning to increase our awareness is a means to enhance our professional practice. Only from a position of self-understanding can we engage learning authentically and holistically through dialogue. On our own journey we inspire the students who model themselves after us and, by example, we encourage a balanced focus on mind, body, and soul.

References

Argyris, C., & Schön, D. A. (1974). *Theory in practice: Increasing professional effectiveness.* San Francisco, CA: Jossey-Bass.

Carse, J. P. (1986). *Finite and infinite games.* New York: Ballantine.

Coalition Against Violence–Avalon East. (n.d.). *The Cycle of Violence.* Available at http://www.coalitionagainstviolence.ca/The%20Cycle%20of%20Violence.htm

Cone, J. G. (2011). Authentic accountability: Tapping the power of the infinite game. J. D. Barbour & G. R. Hickman (Eds.), *Leadership for transformation* (pp. 99–105). San Francisco, CA: Jossey-Bass.

Cook, S. G. (2099, June). Reflection: A key tool for effective leadership. *Women in Higher Education, 18*(6), 1–2.

Covey, S. R. (1989). *The 7 habits of highly effective people: Restoring the character ethic.* New York: Simon & Schuster.

Howe, N., & Strauss, W. (2000). *Millennials rising: The next great generation.* New York: Vintage Books.

Kapur, S. (Director). (2008). *Elizabeth: The golden age* [Motion picture]. United States: NBC Universal Studios.

King, P., & Kitchener, K. S. (1994). *Developing reflective judgment: Understanding and promoting intellectual growth and critical thinking in adolescents and adults.* San Francisco, CA: Jossey-Bass.

Mezirow, J. (1990). *Fostering critical reflection in adulthood: A guide to transformation and emancipatory learning.* San Francisco, CA: Jossey-Bass.

Mezirow, J. (1991). *Transformative dimensions of adult learning.* San Francisco, CA: Jossey-Bass.

Mezirow, J. (2000). Learning to think like an adult: Core concepts of transformation theory. In J. Mezirow (Ed.), *Learning as transformation: Critical perspective on a theory in progress* (pp. 3–33). San Francisco, CA: Jossey-Bass.

Mezirow, J. (2003). *Epistemology of transformative learning.* Unpublished manuscript. Available at http://www.transformativelearning.org/index/Mezirow_EpistemologyTLC.pdf

Perry, W. G., Jr. (1999). *Ethical and intellectual development in the college years: A scheme.* San Francisco, CA: Jossey-Bass. Original work published 1968.

Ruiz, D. M. (1997). *The four agreements: A Toltec wisdom book.* San Rafael, CA: Amber-Allen.

Ruiz, D. M., & Ruiz, D. J. (2010). *The fifth agreement: A practical guide to self-mastery.* San Rafael, CA: Amber-Allen.

Schön, D. A. (1983). *The reflective practitioner: How professionals think in action.* New York: Basic Books.

Schön, D. A. (1987). *Educating the reflective practitioner.* San Francisco, CA: Jossey-Bass.

Yorks, L., & Kasl, E. (2002). Toward a theory and practice for whole-person learning: Reconceptualizing experience and the role of affect. *Adult Education Quarterly, 25*(3), 176–192.

PART THREE

PROFESSIONAL DEVELOPMENT, ACTION RESEARCH, AND SOCIAL AGENCY

7

REFLECTION IN ACTION

Exploring Race and Culture in Critical Reflective Pedagogy

Pamela Petrease Felder

Previous research on the cognitive and social development of college students inside and outside the classroom has addressed the value of racial and cultural awareness and its positive impact on student experience (Heuberger, Gerber, & Anderson, 1999; Hurtado, Milem, Clayton-Pedersen, & Allen, 1998). Two main points drive this discussion: the validity of measuring the impact of diversity on the academic experience for students, and literature on faculty and students that affirms how insensitivity to race and culture continues to be a pervasive issue in our college classrooms (Allen et al. 2002; Antonio et al. 2004; Scheurich & Young, 2002; Villialpando & Delgado Bernal, 2002). Several scholars assert that this insensitivity is a significant factor contributing to a "racial crisis" in American higher education, causing increased underlying racial tension and race-based campus conflicts—particularly for marginalized faculty and students (Allen et al. 2002; Scheurich & Young, 2002; Villialpando & Delgado Bernal, 2002).

Perhaps this "racial crisis" in American higher education is emerging as one of the greatest challenges for members of the college and university community who have an interest in supporting effective diversity initiatives but find it difficult to embrace these initiatives in their teaching. If we are in a crisis in this regard, could those of us who are concerned and actively involved in dealing with issues of racial and cultural awareness be in a state of "racial and cultural crisis management"? For example, when race-based conflicts arise on campus, which members of the academic community are on the forefront in dealing with these conflicts? Specifically, how might faculty members be involved in addressing these conflicts? And, what constitutes a viable response as an effective and proactive approach versus the status quo of racial and cultural crisis management?

As racial and cultural awareness becomes more of a priority in higher education, the functionality of college and university classrooms will depend heavily on faculty members who uphold a commitment to diversity in their teaching and service to the academic community. Yet, beyond commitment, there is a vital need for meaningful action to promulgate this obligation within the classroom environment. Hence, there is a need for a model for teaching race and culture in the classroom.

This chapter will present a model using the teaching narrative as a practical response to the racial crisis in American higher education and is guided by the following questions: How can the teaching narrative serve as a preparation strategy for the teaching of race and culture and the classroom? How can the teaching narrative be used to enhance faculty-student interactions? And, how can it be used for professional development and teaching evaluation? I will address these questions in greater detail in the paragraphs that follow.

The Teaching Narrative as a Critical Reflective Pedagogical Tool

The teaching narrative has become an essential tool in the evaluation of teaching in higher education. There are various methods for using the narrative but very little information about how it can be used to support the teaching of race and culture in higher education. In Bain's (2004) work *What the Best College Teachers Do*, the narrative is discussed as a method for capturing one's "scholarship of teaching" (p. 167). He states,

> a teacher should think about teaching (in a single session or an entire course) as a serious intellectual act, a kind of scholarship, a creation; he or she should then develop a case, complete with evidence, exploring the intellectual (and perhaps artistic) meaning and qualities of that teaching. (p. 169)

Bain's use of the narrative is based in a philosophy that focuses on what the professor "does" in the classroom to enhance student learning (p. 48). A highly valued aspect of his philosophy discussed in the literature on what teachers of race and culture do in the classroom focuses on the development of trust between the faculty member and the students. This is consistent with hooks's (1994) transgressive teaching ideology that underscores a commitment to facilitating meaningful and effective interactions among faculty and students where the process of learning subject matter is developed with trust and respect. Although consideration of student learning is a basic tenet of the transmission model (teachers transmitting knowledge to students), trust and respect may not be considered priorities of the teaching process, particularly as they relate to building faculty-student relationships. In terms of the lack of trust and respect in the college classroom being a contributing factor to the racial crisis in American higher education, Hurtado (1992) asserts that faculty members have a critical role in improving campus climates. She asserts:

> To improve the climate research suggests that institutions can create environments with relatively low racial/ethnic tension or conflict if they are attentive to a variety of issues related to diversity and if faculty and administrators demonstrate a general concern for student development. (p. 560)

This notion is consistent with Bain's (2004) assessment of evaluating teaching strategies. He is clear to delineate that the skill of developing trust with students is a characteristic associated with the best teaching practices. He states,

> Professors who established special trust with their students often displayed a kind of openness in which they might, from time to time, talk about their intellectual journey, its ambitions, triumphs, frustrations, and failures, and encourage students to be similarly reflective and candid. (p. 141)

Bain's assessment of what professors do has a unique implication for those who teach race and culture and takes on a different meaning when contextualized in the teaching of race and culture. For the professor who teaches race and culture as the core subject, his or her racial and/or cultural worldview has the grave potential to be the focal point of every message delivered to students inside and outside of the classroom. In fact, some might argue that a professor's race and/or culture could be significant factors to those students who prioritize racial centrality as a valued aspect of their intellectual identity development and performance.

This work acknowledges that teaching race and culture can be considered controversial by many professors in the academy, and an aversion to teaching these topics could be based on the principle that these issues are not relevant to their subject matter. Some argue this is not conducive to learning environments for those students who value race and culture in their learning experience. Certainly, such arguments highlight a volatile source for potential racial conflict and crisis and underscore the need for a teaching model on race and culture.

In their discussion of preparing for distance education courses in higher education McKeachie and Svinicki (2006) suggest that the teaching narrative should be a "storyline" to support the delivery of a theoretical argument in teaching (p. 294). The storyline focus aspect of the narrative facilitates student thinking toward new concepts as the course progresses. The narrative becomes a resource teachers use to make meaning of the faculty-student interaction, whereby "teachers lend students the capacity to construct meanings they cannot yet achieve unaided" (McKeachie & Svinicki, 2006, p. 294). Thus, the value a professor lends to his or her personal understanding about race and culture becomes the driving force for supporting student learning during the course.

Although Bain (2004) and McKeachie and Svinicki (2006) consistently address the important role students play in the development of the teaching narrative, there is very little discussion of the faculty member or students' racial and cultural experiences. Ideas about the impact of race and culture must be inferred by the reader or gleaned from their discussion of developing the teaching narrative; they are not explicit. Furthermore, in the discussion of teaching philosophies, the treatment of students, or the evaluation of teaching, there is no discussion of how a teacher's racial and cultural worldviews could influence faculty-student relationships in the classroom.

Bain's (2004) and McKeachie and Svinicki's (2006) work prompts consideration of how the teaching narrative can be used to facilitate faculty-student interactions that involve race and culture. Because of this, this work explores the use of the teaching narrative and how it can serve to facilitate awareness of racial and cultural issues among students in the classroom. Moreover, there is a discussion of how the teaching narrative can be used as a faculty professional development instrument that facilitates metacognitive analysis and self-reflection about one's teaching.

Included in Bain's (2004) and McKeachie and Svinicki's (2006) work is an example of a teaching narrative that embraces a personal commitment to presenting issues of race and culture as a transformational element of teaching within an elite graduate school context. This narrative operationalizes a philosophy that prioritizes the meaning-making experience for both faculty and students as it relates to race and culture.

If a professor's goal is to instruct students about race and culture, a critical element of the extrapolation process is the professor developing and maintaining a critical personal awareness of racial and cultural issues from a multidimensional perspective. Therefore, this model's approach to enacting students' learning of race and culture as a liberating practice begins with the teaching narrative. The written narrative is the focal point for extrapolating elements of this liberating process. It allows the teacher to place issues of race and culture as the central focus of his or her teaching preparation, along with execution and reflection of the teaching practice.

Transgressive Pedagogy: Embracing the Negotiation of Trust in the Classroom

In their work "Negotiating Power, Developing Trust: Transgressing Race and Status in the Academy," Gasman, Gerstl-Pepin, Anderson-Thompkins, Rasheed, and Hathaway (2004) address how faculty members see the centrality of race and culture as a priority in the classroom. The underlying premise for this work is the authors' commitment to reshaping faculty-student interactions to enhance institutional climates for marginalized students. Using narrative inquiry by way of faculty and doctoral student collaboration, the authors share their belief systems about issues of race and culture as they relate to building trust among faculty and students. Specifically, they explore the experiences of African American doctoral students and the impact of race and status in the academy. In contrasting the experiences of students who felt valued in the academic environment to those who felt like "casualties of war," they determined that there are many unspoken assumptions about race that negatively affect the inclusion of students of color and White faculty members with shared values. To illustrate this inclusive philosophy via teaching perspectives, two faculty members share their belief systems about the value of race and culture in the academy. Marybeth states,

> I think it is crucial that we as faculty members offer nurturing experiences if we are to provide a collegial environment for students that is reflective of their backgrounds. (Gasman et al., 2004, p. 694).

Similarly, Cindy asserts:

> I was fortunate to work with a diverse group of students who challenged me to see the ways in which the academy can constitute an oppressive space—for example, how Westernized forms of knowledge are privileged. Opening my eyes to the subtle forms of discrimination that permeated seemingly benign classroom issues—such as the selected reading, pedagogical style, methods of assessment, and which viewpoints are privileged—made me aware of the power that faculty members wield. This awareness now permeates my teaching and interactions with graduate students. (Gasman, et al., 2004, p. 694)

Both of these faculty members see racial and cultural awareness as a central aspect of their teaching. Moreover, there is specific reference to how this awareness is connected to pedagogical strategies inside the classroom. Additionally, their commitment to building strong student-faculty relationships appears to be central to their teaching, as the students in their study also embrace this ideology (Gasman et al., 2004). Their perspective advances hooks's (1994) notion of transgressive pedagogy that conceptualizes the influence a marginalized treatment of topics and the facilitation of classroom interactions can have (Gasman et al., 2004). Hooks (1994) describes her philosophy of engaged pedagogy and relates it to the responsibility of teaching in a multicultural world:

> To educate as the practice of freedom is a way of teaching that anyone can learn. That learning process comes easiest to those of us who teach who also believe that our work is not merely to share information but to share in the intellectual and spiritual growth of our students. To teach in a manner that respects and cares for the souls of our students is essential if we are to provide the necessary conditions where learning can most deeply and intimately begin. (p. 13)

A powerful aspect of hooks's vision on teaching is her focus on the sacred obligation teachers have in caring for their students. One conclusion drawn from hooks's work is that a liberating teaching experience must involve some balance of facilitating both academic and spiritual growth.

The quotes from both Marybeth and Cindy (Gasman et al., 2004) illustrate how this liberation process is based in a reflective orientation that serves to uplift the academic environment. This orientation not only supports the students, but also serves to enrich the experiences of the teachers. Each of the quotes speaks to how the teachers' lives are enriched either by way of an enhanced collegial environment, or through their broadened views of student experiences within the context of oppressive educational systems. Marybeth's and Cindy's narratives juxtaposed with hooks's points about teaching as a practice of freedom raise an interesting question: How do teachers provide classroom environments that are reflective of students' backgrounds to foster a liberating teaching experience? How does this liberation process begin with the development of the teaching narrative?

In the academy the teaching of race and culture still remains on the periphery of core curriculum programming. For example, diversity courses in higher education graduate programs are offered as electives and not considered core requirements for graduation. Given the presence of racial and cultural issues in the academy (and other levels of the educational spectrum), teaching students to be culturally competent for a rapidly changing student demographic should be a priority for institutions that aim to be responsive to student needs (Wallace, 2000). One way to increase the presence of race and culture in the teaching experience within the academy is to incorporate research on these issues into the development of the teaching narrative.

For example, for teachers who are looking to embrace a liberation philosophy in the classroom, Milner's (2007) ideology about the responsibility researchers have to maintain integrity when interpreting and representing communities of color could be applied within a teaching context. His work addresses questions that should be raised when conducting research on communities of color to avoid potential conflicts or dangers that arise when race and culture is not considered. Placed within the context of developing a teaching narrative, these questions serve to facilitate thought about how race and culture can be addressed in one's teaching. Some of Milner's (2007) questions (modified with a focus on teaching) include:

- What is the contextual nature of race, racism and culture in my teaching? In other words, what do race, racism, and culture mean in the community under study and in the broader community? How do I know?
- What is known socially, institutionally, and historically about the community and people under study? In other words, what does my curriculum reveal about the racial or cultural issue(s) under discussion? How do I know? (p. 397).

Consulting this research (by asking several questions previously mentioned) can influence teachers to think about their racial and cultural worldviews and how they are incorporated into their teaching. Moreover, themes for thinking about how race and culture could be addressed in the development of faculty-student relationships are identified using a modified version of Bain's (2004) four fundamental inquiries for creating successful learning environments. They include: (a) What should my students be able to do intellectually, physically, emotionally as a result of their learning? (b) How can I encourage those abilities and the habits of the heart and mind to use them? (c) How do I attempt to understand the nature, quality, and progress of my students' learning? (d) How do I evaluate my efforts to foster that learning? (p. 49). The confluence of Milner's and Bain's questions creates a framework for exploring the use of racial and cultural elements in the preparation, execution, and evaluation of teaching focused on supporting faculty-student interaction and teacher self-reflection.

The Method

In discussing the practical advantages of using qualitative methods to conduct formative evaluations Maxwell (2005) asserts: "In such evaluations, it is more important to understand the process by which things happen in a particular situation than to rigorously compare this situation with others" (p. 24). Moreover, Creswell (1998) suggests that a basic axiom for users of narrative inquiry is the consciousness of the audience in the researchers' thought process—hence the narrative tradition used, as it supports the instructor in gauging how racial and cultural aspects in teaching are embraced by the students.

The Design of a Critical Reflective Pedagogical Tool

Tillman's (2005) Generative Evaluation Model for conducting culturally sensitive research is the method used to assess a teaching narrative in my study. This evaluation design is flexible in identifying the methodology itself as a cultural artifact in the process of teaching race and culture and was developed to evaluate a "culturally nurturing pedagogical experience" (p. 313). Furthermore, the narrative is explored through various components of the teaching process (i.e., preparation, execution, evaluation; p. 315).

Data Collection

The narrative selected for this chapter was developed by an African American female faculty member who taught a higher education diversity course within an elite graduate school of education. The course objective was to teach models of race and culture as they relate to different functional areas of the college and university environment. The narrative represents the faculty member's general belief systems about the development of the course and perspectives about faculty-student interactions.

Triangulation is used as the primary method of analysis. "This strategy reduces the risk that your conclusions will reflect only the systematic biases or limitations of a specific source or method, and allows you to gain a broader and more secure understanding of the issues you are investigating" (Maxwell, 2005, p. 94). The sources of data include the teaching narrative, previous research on the teaching of race and culture from a faculty of color perspective, teacher notes and journals, assigned readings for the topic under discussion, and classroom observation notes (including questions and comments from students).

Through the process of answering Milner's (2007) and Bain's (2004) questions, the narrative is analyzed to generate a culturally sensitive evaluation of teaching and offers perspectives on minimizing racial conflict, serving to address the racial crisis discussed earlier.

Data Analysis

Six procedures guide the analysis of the teaching narrative. Tillman's (2005) research primarily focuses on generating group evaluations. However, this narrative evaluation is developed from an individualistic perspective to facilitate self-reflection. Thus, the procedures have been modified for individual use and include using collective and individual cultural perspective as an analytical lens; identifying, collecting, and analyzing data using multiple perspectives; providing opportunities for graduate students to dialogue with one another; maintaining an awareness of and sensitivity to graduate students' career and psychosocial needs related to their growth and development; seeking cross-cultural views by interviewing and engaging participants from diverse races/ethnicities; and posing questions that are directly related to the lived experience/reality in the academy.

Example of a Teaching Narrative

During a 15-week semester I arrive to class 15–20 minutes before the scheduled start time to set the tone for the class. I've noticed that the graduate students at my institution arrive to class early. Often I bring a cup of coffee and brief journal articles (one-page) regarding the session topic and speak to students about their perspectives. As other students arrive, they join the discussion. I find when students are engaged with each other before class they are likely to engage themselves by taking exploratory risks during class. Taking risks is essential for fostering "flexibility and forgiveness" in class discussions. Once "flexibility and forgiveness" is established an intellectual community manifests where thoughts are liberated among its members (Walker, Golde, Jones, Bueschel, & Hutchings, 2008). This pre-class interaction also serves to tear down formal barriers of authority and makes students feel comfortable especially at the beginning of the semester (Gasman et al. 2004).

I see my role as a professor in the graduate classroom as a facilitator of my student's professional development. Most of my students are master's-level graduate students with an interest in becoming student affairs practitioners. I inform them that developing cultural competence is becoming increasingly important within college and university environments and awareness about racial and cultural issues is the first step to developing this competence. To facilitate psychosocial growth I employ exercises that foster metacognitive analysis on students' worldviews about race and culture. The guiding question for this exercise is: "Why do you hold your beliefs about race and cultures?" Subquestions about class, familial background and influences, spirituality, and politics are conceptually driven in discussion, and students are encouraged to write about these perspectives in journals to maintain sensitivity (Heuberger et al., 1999).

Milner's (2007) study is integral in this facilitation, because it includes questions students can ask when conducting work on races and cultures other than their own. Additionally, I encourage students to think about these questions from both a theoretical and a behavioral standpoint. In other words, I ask students to ponder about a "seen danger" associated with not asking the right questions and then ask them to think about a situation where a similar instance occurred (Milner, 2007). Or, I encourage them to think about an active illustration. In some cases we may engage in role play. From a scholarly standpoint, I encourage my students to develop a respect for the body of scholarship about race and cultural awareness. Taliaferro Baszile's (2004) work serves to contextualize a perspective of a Black female professor in higher education. The Black female professor is a minority within elite institutions, which lends an example of status oppression in the academy and challenges associated with negotiating success. Although I may not ascribe to all of the ideologies in Taliaferro Baszile's experience, my representation in the classroom associates me with the author's perspective racially and culturally. I've observed that students are curious to know if my ideologies are the same as the author's. I see this collective curiosity as an opportunity to allow students to ask me questions about my experience as a Black female professor in an elite institutional environment. I set discussion criteria where students are encouraged to ask any question, and I respond introspectively.

A recurring theme for my instruction is self-reflection. Because many of these students are student affairs practitioners or are preparing for work in the field, students are encouraged to explore this commitment via their collegiate classroom experiences by way of a self-reflective journal assignment and to explore the following statements/questions: Explain your most significant undergraduate classroom experience. How would you identify the diversity in that classroom (racial, cultural, socioeconomic)? Did you perceive the presence/lack of diversity to foster/hinder your academic experience? How has that influenced how you view race and culture in the classroom?

Limitations of Developing Teaching Narratives

The goal of this work is to support the development of teaching narratives focused on *understanding* race and culture in the classroom. Its underlying premise is to facilitate teacher self-reflection. Thus, the narrative and analysis represented herein should be viewed as a guidance model for self-initiated narrative development and evaluation.

Teaching Narrative Analysis

In this section I draw connections among aspects of the narrative, literature, and reflections about teaching racial and cultural issues. The contextual nature of race and culture represented in the narrative is illustrated by the conviction the faculty member holds about racial and cultural uplift in the field of higher education. From this faculty member's perspective, learning about race and culture is valued as both theoretical and practical. This is exemplified in the following statement: "I inform them that developing cultural competence is becoming increasingly important within college and university environments and awareness about racial and cultural issues is the first step to developing this competence." This statement also addresses the faculty member's belief systems and expectations about what her students should be able to do intellectually, physically, and emotionally as a result of their learning.

The faculty member identifies that the students being taught are interested in the field of higher education in terms of addressing the question, "What do race, racism and culture mean in the community under study and in the broader community? How do I know?" (Milner, 2007, p. 397). Narrative contextualizes the role of student affairs practitioners in higher education by introducing a historical factor of the profession and its relation to the value of culture in higher education. This statement underscores that learning about race and culture is the precursor to one's behavioral capacity to be committed to preserving and transmitting cultural competence. hooks (1994) might assert that this is a transgressive feature of the narrative.

In discussing what is known socially, institutionally, and historically about the community under study, the following narrative statement makes specific mention of racial and cultural issues regarding faculty in the academy. In particular a book chapter is used in one of her class sessions. This book chapter speaks to the Black female faculty member experience and the narrative mentions that some of the experiences in this literature may facilitate curiosity among students about the narrator's own racial and cultural experience.

Milner's research underscores the importance of asking questions to learn more about one's personal racial and cultural identity in an effort to be aware of other racial and cultural perspectives. In this aspect of the narrative, the faculty member encourages student curiosity by allowing her to ask questions about her own experience as a Black faculty member. According to Bain's (2004) work, this encouragement fosters the capacity to ask questions pertaining to racial and cultural issues, critical habits of heart and mind in developing cultural competence.

Additionally, the narrative addresses how the faculty member attempts to understand the nature, quality, and progress of students' learning through role play and active illustration by stating, "In some cases we may engage in role play." It's not clear what these cases are, nor is there any discussion about how students are being formally evaluated. However, it is important to note that the faculty member also uses other forms of evaluating student work, including student papers, weekly journal assignments, and student presentations.

The narrative incorporates multiple research perspectives to corroborate with the faculty member's approach to teaching. There are opportunities for both faculty and graduates to dialogue outside of the formal class time. The pre-class discussion exemplifies this faculty-student interaction. The narrative documents an awareness of the graduate students' career and psychosocial needs, as indicated by the pre-class discussion, emphasis on professional development, and attention to developing open faculty-student dialogue. And cross-cultural views are sought by the incorporation of relevant research.

Tillman's (2005) methodology includes posing questions that are directly related to the participants' "lived" experiences in the academy (Tillman, 2005, p. 315). The lived experience as a faculty woman of color is explored through the process of responding to the modified version of Milner's (2007) questions that explore the faculty member's racial and cultural positionality.

It's important to note that the use of Milner's questions is one example of how culturally based research can be used to facilitate culturally sensitive teaching. Certainly, other types of racially and culturally based research could be used. Many of the sources used in this paper could be consulted for that purpose. Milner's questions are highly recommended, because they are geared to minimize conflict between the researcher and the population being studied. Similarly, using them in a teaching context can help teachers see the "dangers arise particularly when researchers do not consider, negotiate, balance, and attend to the complex nature of race and culture in their research" (Milner, 2007, p. 392). Again, avoiding these dangers reduces the risk for racial conflict, therefore serving to address the racial crisis that exists within our colleges and universities.

A Model for Teaching Race and Culture

The process to generate a self-evaluation of one's teaching of race and culture might be considered very similar to the way that many professors prepare for a lecture. It's not uncommon to learn that a professor uses lecture notes that may be updated from time to time. The distinct characteristic about this model is its focus on the use of racially and culturally based material in the teaching process. For instance, a biology professor may introduce curriculum about the life cycle, but how does the professor make it racially and culturally relevant?

Based on the narrative evaluation presented earlier, a model for teaching race and culture was developed based on four emerging themes: personal commitment to social justice, classroom management, facilitation of conversations on racial and cultural topics, and self-evaluation of teaching efforts. These themes specifically address how faculty members can minimize racial conflict in the classroom.

Personal Commitment to Social Justice

The narrative speaks to the professor's encouraging students to develop an intellectual awareness about different races and culture. This awareness may lead to a greater understanding (e.g., a greater level of consciousness when reading or writing about racial and cultural topics) and in some cases a behavioral change (e.g., joining institutional groups, learning more about this topic outside of class, or simply treating someone with a renewed sensitivity about race) (Baxter-Magolda, 1992).

Classroom Management

Encouraging each student's ability is tied to each professor's classroom management style. Previous literature on teaching race and culture in the classroom discusses the value of classroom management in addressing conflict and negotiation (Heuberger et al., 1999). In discussing classroom interactions regarding race and culture, Heuberger et al. (1999) state, "Conflict may be viewed as a natural result of interaction among people of different cultures. But at the same time, we know that human beings enjoy a unique capacity for understanding" (p. 108).

Negotiating conflict is an important skill for facilitating class discussion. However, when teaching issues of race and culture, the potential conflict is greater, because students may feel personal conflicts about embracing various ideologies about race and culture. For example, if a teacher is discussing the status of systemic oppression in the educational system, students may be victims of the oppression who have never had the opportunity to express the experience of victimization. An instructor must be skilled at acknowledging the emotion associated with that student's sense of marginalization, but should work to facilitate the emotion associated with that experience in a constructive manner. One way to do this is to provide opportunities for the student's expression and to ask guided questions to connect that experience to the material discussed in the course. Also, this guidance should not be limited to in-class instruction. Students should be given the opportunity to channel this expression outside of the classroom in student-faculty meetings and via individual assignments like weekly journal entries (Heuberger et al., 1999).

Facilitation of Conversations on Racial and Cultural Topics

To evaluate the quality and nature of student learning about race and culture, facilitating conversations around the course subject matter should be supported with activities outside of the classroom (Gasman et al., 2004). The platform for the discipline of learning about race and culture can begin with discussions in the classroom, but the deconstruction and construction of the ideas that takes place in class must extend to activities beyond that traditional setting. Often there is a curiosity that accompanies the development of awareness about these issues, and often students want to know if their interpretations of the material are valid or invalid. Therefore, there should be other venues outside of the classroom where students can address their curiosity.

In addition to weekly journals, professors may want to facilitate scholarly symposia for the institutional community, where students and other members of that community can discuss issues of race and culture. Also, student-faculty interaction should be encouraged through the use of a professor's office hours, and if there are other institutional community events focused on race and culture, professors should consider including the attendance of those events as requirements for the course.

Self-Evaluation of Teaching Efforts

There is very little research about the evaluation of teaching race and culture in the classroom. This self-evaluation process discussed in this paper provides a model for continual self-development and improvement in teaching race and culture. Future use of this model may be used to generate group evaluations of teaching to facilitate discussions among faculty who are interested in promoting racial and cultural awareness. The themes presented in this paper should not be viewed in the light of being right or wrong. Rather, they are suggestive and provide guidance for professors who are interested in a self-evaluative assessment of their teaching strategies.

In keeping with hooks's concept of creating conditions in the classroom, "where learning can most deeply and intimately begin," the model presented here embraces the ideology that profound learning experiences are likely to occur when the teacher makes an effort to learn from his or her teaching process (hooks, 1994, p. 8). Transgressive pedagogy by way of self-evaluation can be a profound learning experience for the teacher and an opportunity to determine how to maximize the opportunity to present issues of race and culture.

Conclusion

Through the process of conducting this research, a few conclusions and questions about teaching self-evaluation using the teaching narrative were drawn and considered. First, the teaching narrative is an essential aspect of the teaching evaluation process and offers a platform for faculty members to explore their perspectives about race and culture. Furthermore, using the narrative can serve to broaden a faculty member's consciousness regarding race and culture and how they are included in the classroom environment. Again, Milner's framework is the basis for asking, "How do you know what the nature of race is in one's teaching?" Triangulation allows for critical assessment of the teacher's self-perception about race and how that perception might be viewed within the classroom environment and considers how that perception is relevant to race and culture research literature. It also serves as a record for how faculty-student interactions were fostered, developed, and nurtured. Future research should consider how narratives can continue to be used to address how these interactions are evaluated, to learn more about the transgressive teaching process.

Second, the teaching narrative lends a contextual framework to one's belief systems about race and how they might be manifested through the curriculum. Although teachers may understand these concepts by way of a personal commitment to social justice, the narrative facilitates thinking about how that commitment is translated into the selection of readings, classroom management, the facilitation of class discussion, faculty-student interaction, and ongoing collegial discussions about the value of diversity in the academy.

Third, the teaching narrative can serve as a professional development tool for teachers of race and culture who may need both personal and scholarly support within their institutions. The teaching narrative could be used more consistently within the academy to broaden formal discussions about racial and cultural awareness among faculty members who are interested in social justice issues. The evaluation of the narrative presented herein was developed from an individual perspective. However, these narratives could be part of a group evaluation where faculty members who teach race and culture could evaluate each other's narratives.

Finally, the teaching narrative could be used for every class during a semester, less frequently at varying intervals during the semester, or just once at the beginning of the semester. The overarching idea of the model is to encourage teachers to think about the teaching of race and culture comprehensively by incorporating racially and culturally based research and evaluation in the teaching process with some level of consistency.

References

Allen, W. R., Epps, E. G., Guillory, E. A., Suh, S. A., Bonous-Hammarth, M., & Stassen, M. L. A. (2002). Outsiders within: Race, gender, and faculty status in U.S. higher education. In W. A. Smith, P. G. Altbach, & K. Lomotey (Eds.), *The racial crisis in American higher education: Continuing challenges for the twenty-first century* (pp. 189–220). New York: State University of New York Press.

Altbach, P. (2005). Patterns in higher education development. In, P. G. Altbach, R. O. Berdahl, & P. Gumport (Eds.), *American higher education in the twenty-first century: social, political, and economic challenges* (pp. 15–37). Baltimore, MD: The Johns Hopkins University Press.

Antonio, A. L., Chang, M. J., Hakuta, K., Kenny, D. A., Levin, S., & Milem, J. F. (2004). Effects of racial diversity on complex thinking in college students. *Psychological Science, 15*(8), 507–510.

Bain, K. (2004). *What the best college teachers do.* Boston, MA: Harvard University Press.

Baxter-Magolda, M. B. (1992). *Knowing and reasoning in college: Gender-related patterns in students' intellectual development.* San Francisco, CA: Jossey-Bass.

Creswell, J. (1998). Qualitative inquiry and research design: Choosing among five traditions. Thousand Oaks, CA: Sage.

Gasman, M. (2006). Who's biased now? *The Chronicle of Higher Education, 52*(43), B5.

Gasman, M., Gerstl-Pepin, C., Anderson-Thompkins, S., Rasheed, L., & Hathaway, K. (2004). Negotiating power, developing trust: Transgressing race and status in the academy. *Teachers College Record, 106*(4), 689–715.

Heuberger, B., Gerber, D., & Anderson, R. (1999). Strength through cultural diversity: Developing and teaching a diversity course. *College Teaching, 7*(3), 107–113.

hooks, b. (1994). *Teaching to transgress: Education as a practice of freedom.* New York: Routledge.

Hurtado, S. (1992). The campus racial climate: Contexts of conflict. *Journal of Higher Education, 35*(1), 539–569.

Hurtado, S., Milem, J., Clayton-Pedersen, A. R., & Allen, W. R. (1998). Enhancing campus climates for racial/ethnic diversity: Educational policy and practice. *The Review of Higher Education, 21*(3), 279–302.

Maxwell, J. A. (2005). *Qualitative research design: An interactive approach* (2nd ed.). Thousand Oaks, CA: Sage.

McKeachie, W. J., & Svinicki, M. (2006). *McKeachie's teaching tips: Strategies, research, and theory for college and university teachers.* Boston, MA: Houghton-Mifflin.

Milner, H. R. (2007). Race, culture, and researcher positionality: Working through dangers seen, unseen, and unforeseen. *Educational Researcher, 36*(7), 338–400.

Scheurich, J. J., & Young, M. (2002). White racism among White faculty: From critical understanding to antiracist activism. In W. A. Smith, P. G. Altbach, & K. Lomotey (Eds.), *The racial crisis in American higher education: Continuing challenges for the twenty-first century* (pp. 221–242). New York: State University of New York Press.

Taliaferro Baszile, D. M. (2004). "Who does she think she is?": Growing up nationalist and ending up teaching race in White space. In D. Cleveland (Ed.), *A long way to go: Conversations about race by African American faculty and graduate students* (pp. 158–170). New York: Peter Lang.

Tillman, L. (2005). Culturally sensitive research and evaluation: Advancing an agenda for Black education. In J. King (Ed.), *Black education: A transformative research and action agenda for the new century* (pp. 313–321). Mahwah, NJ: Lawrence Erlbaum Associates.

Villialpando, O., & Delgado Bernal, D. (2002). A critical race theory analysis of barriers that impede the success of faculty of color. In W. A. Smith, P. G. Altbach, & K. Lomotey (Eds.), *The racial crisis in American higher education: Continuing challenges for the twenty-first century* (pp. 243–270). New York: State University of New York Press.

Walker, G. E., Golde, C. M., Jones, L., Bueschel, A. C., & Hutchings, P. (2008). The formation of scholars: *Rethinking doctoral education for the twenty-first century*. San Francisco, CA: The Carnagie Foundation for the Advancement of Teaching. Jossey-Bass Publishing.

Wallace, B. C. (2000). A call for change in multicultural training at graduate schools of education: Educating to end oppression and for social justice. *Teachers College Record, 102*(6), 1086–1111.

8

TEACHING PROFESSIONAL DEVELOPMENT IN HIGHER EDUCATION AND STUDENT AFFAIRS

Unless

Stacy A. Jacob

"Unless someone like you cares a whole awful lot, nothing is going to get better. It's not." —Dr. Seuss, 1971, p. 58

Each time I teach a capstone course for new, soon-to-be recipients of master's degrees and future higher education student affairs professionals, I am confronted with, through my students, the job market for new professionals. I get worried questions from my students: "Do I know enough?" "Am I ready?" "What is my new job going to expect from me?"

I answer them with, "You do not know enough, you are not ready, and your new job is going to expect from you more than you can deliver."

As their eyes widen with shock, I look off into the distance and say, "Unless . . ."

And here begins what I consider the most important series of conversations I will have with my students before they enter the workforce.

Graduate course work in student affairs programs teaches students many important things such as the history that undergirds the system in which we work, the theories of student development that guide us in helping students succeed in and out of the college classroom, and the ways in which we can collect information so that we can make data-driven decisions. However, we largely overlook the professional development of our future student affairs practitioners—after all, professional development is largely something that happens after us. We can also be guilty of not providing students with sufficient opportunities to reflect on and integrate the theories we teach into practice, and, in doing so, we fail to help our students understand that to

121

thrive in a profession that seeks to serve others, we must first know ourselves critically, and knowing ourselves means taking time to reflect. For how can we nurture others through change unless we, too, are willing to learn and grow in our profession? Often what we fail to teach our students is how to create paths for themselves that can lead to actionable change, both within themselves and for our institutions.

What Is Professional Development?

To fully understand professional development, it is first important to define what it means to be a professional. Carpenter and Stimpson (2007) explain the development of the term *professional* by tracing three areas in which scholars have attempted to define it: via traits that professionals have in common, the process a person goes through to become a professional, and the way the term *professional* is used to represent various occupations. Carpenter and Stimpson (2007) build on the work of Brint (1993), Friedson (1986), and Pavalko (1971) to define *profession* as a field that "should require a high degree of specialized knowledge and skill, be based primarily upon service motivation, should concern a crucial societal task or tasks, and should require an extended preparation among other things" (p. 268). The authors then discuss if student affairs can be a profession and come to the conclusion that, although the field does not strictly adhere to all definitions, for practical purposes, it can be considered a profession (Carpenter & Stimpson, 2007). Although this discourse may seem like intellectual pontificating, it is important to understand that many people inside and outside of the academy may not perceive student affairs as a legitimate profession. Therefore, it is incumbent on our field to ensure that we are seen as competent educators within our colleges and universities.

To ensure that we are seen as competent and to best serve our students, we must be engaged in a lifelong process of growth and improvement. We must continually expand our skills and competencies through professional development. Schreiber, Dunkel, and Jahr (1994) define professional development as "involvement in activities that are intended to enhance professional effectiveness, and are chosen as a result of a decision-making process based on assessment of skills and designed goals while targeting skill development" (p. 26). Therefore, professional development is one part skill assessment and one part personal decision making.

Although professional development relies heavily on an individual's unique needs, it is important to understand that for student affairs practitioners, growth stems from far more than a personal dedication to it. Our obligation to professional development is explicitly called for by our two largest professional organizations, the American College Personnel Association

(ACPA) and the National Association of Student Personnel Administrators (NASPA). ACPA's *Statement of Ethical Principles and Standards* (2006) notes in standard 1.3 that members should "maintain and enhance professional effectiveness by continually improving skills and acquiring new knowledge." NASPA's *Standards of Professional Practice* (1990) also emphasizes the importance of professional development in standard 17, saying,

> Members have an obligation to continue personal professional growth and to contribute to the development of the profession by enhancing personal knowledge and skills, sharing ideas and information, improving professional practices, conducting and reporting research, and participating in association activities.

So a commitment to professional development, although individual, extends beyond a requirement to ourselves; it is also an obligation to our students, our institutions, and our field.

Reflection and Professional Development

Quite simply, in order for professionals to assess their skills and create a plan for improvement, they need to understand themselves well. Reflection provides one of the best paths toward an understanding of oneself. Although reflection is a critical skill for growth and learning, it is not a skill that most new professionals are trained in or possess. In a fast-paced world filled with technology that provides continuous distractions, multiple and pervasive entertainment opportunities, and a culture of constant connection, we all lack the silence, time, and space needed to reflect. Because of this, new professionals may need help in claiming time for themselves to develop lifelong reflection skills.

How Can We Teach Students in Our Student Affairs Preparation Programs to Reflect?

Reflection is not a natural act for all students, and aiding them in finding the intrinsic motivation for reflection can be one way that graduate programs in higher education and student affairs assist new professionals in bridging the gap between what they have learned in graduate school and what they need to know to be successful professionals. Reflection can facilitate professionals understanding themselves in deep and meaningful ways that lead to growth, learning, and change. But how can faculty help students engage, buy in, and actually do reflection? Further, how can faculty assist students in moving beyond a reflection that is a self-centered set of musings (akin to status updates on Facebook) to a consistent activity that helps students critique and understand themselves in order to promote better awareness of themselves and the effects of their actions and use this critical reflection for growth and change?

Many students in student affairs master's programs come to preparation programs right after an undergraduate degree, having just "discovered" the field. Most have not thought much about how higher education works or how student affairs practitioners work within higher education. Learning about our professional standards, philosophies, how colleges are organized, student development theories, and more can be overwhelming, and somewhere in the process, they can lose who they are and what they believe. Reminding students that they are also in a developmental process is an important role for faculty. At times we push them to the cognitive dissonance that leads them to higher order thinking as we are teaching them about student development. It is not enough to let our students believe that they are learning about student development in others; we must help them see that they are also on a developmental path. When we teach critical reflection, we help show students where they are, so they can design paths for growth.

Classroom Exercises for Reflection

The following sections describe classroom activities and exercises I have found useful in helping students learn to critically reflect and use that reflection to determine both the paths they might choose to take in the future and the areas in which they feel they have a need to grow.

In Praise of Journaling

Journaling is an excellent way to find out about yourself, how you react to situations, your interactions with people, and other workplace-related skills and competencies. If you honestly write about yourself, your struggles, your successes and failures, and situations in the workplace, journaling documents your growth and learning over time and aids in understanding yourself better. Students who look over their journal entries are often surprised to note that common themes arise over and over, and these themes speak volumes about who they are, what they may need to work on, and their passions within the field. In essence, a journal can provide a student with "research" about themselves. Reflexive journaling is an established tradition in qualitative research (Ortlipp, 2008), and, therefore, making the leap from treating a journal as personal musings to a store of data that can be analyzed to reveal information about the writer is a reasonable practice. However, using journals in this manner does not usually occur to students, nor do they necessarily know how to begin writing a journal that can be of use to their growth and learning.

Helping students learn to reflect in a journal can provide them the means by which they autonomously explore themselves as professionals and develop plans for their professional growth. But how can we, as faculty in professional preparation programs in student affairs and higher education, teach the skill of journaling for professional growth? First and foremost, we must introduce students to the idea of journaling as personal data. We can talk about journaling with this approach, suggest it, and require it as part of our courses. One good way to help students start thinking about journaling is to ask new student advisees to keep a journal of all the things that interest them and the questions that arise from their interests in their classes. I generally refer to this as a research journal with my advisees. I suggest students keep a research journal as a way to find ideas for class papers, projects, theses, and dissertations.

In courses, we can teach the skill of journaling by providing prompts, offering readings that may cause reflection, and asking students to react to certain materials in class. Personally, I find journaling an excellent way to begin class. It demarcates the end of the outside world and the start of the world inside our class, warms up our brains, and provides a way to initiate discussion. Some texts that I find intriguing to help think about life, life journey, and professional development are *The Alchemist* (Coelho, 2006); *College Organization and Professional Development: Integrating Moral Reasoning and Reflective Practice* (St. John, 2009); *Fables, Labels, and Folding Tables: Reflections on the Student Affairs Profession* (Mitchell, 1999); and *Listen Very Loud: Paying Attention in the Student Affairs Profession* (Mitchell, 2001). The St. John text and the Mitchell texts provide prompts for reflection.

Left-Column Exercise

The left-column exercise (referred to elsewhere in this book, though not by this specific title), which was originally conceived of by Argyris and Schön (1974) and was used in St. John's (2009) work and teachings, is an excellent tool to help students discover if what they believe about how they should act is congruent with how they behave. Argyris and Schön (1974) use "espoused theory" and "theory-in-use" to explain "the theory that actually governs his actions is his theory-in-use, which may or may not be compatible with his espoused theory" (p. 7). They then appropriately point out that "the individual may or may not be aware of the incompatibility of the two theories" (Argyris & Schön, 1974, p. 7). In other words, professionals often do not act in a manner that matches what they say they believe—student affairs professionals are, of course, not exempt from this problem. Incongruence between beliefs and actions is highly problematic and can make a professional seem to lack integrity.

As faculty, we teach the theories, principles, and values that many student affairs practitioners come to espouse, and, because of this, we have vested interest in our students using those theories, principles, and values to guide their action. Use of the left-column exercise helps us illustrate to our students if they are being congruent. Understanding the incongruence is helpful to helping the student grow professionally in our field.

The left-column exercise uses a dialogue or series of dialogues in which the student has participated. Students split a page into two columns. In the right column, students write out a dialogue they have had in a professional setting. In the left column and in correspondence with the dialogue, students write out what they were thinking (honestly) as the conversation progressed. The dialogue(s) then become evidence through which students can analyze their behavior, and class time can be used to discuss and debrief incongruence between espoused beliefs and theories-in-use.

The Lorax

The Lorax (Dr. Seuss, 1971) is one of my favorite children's books. Although it is an environmental tale, its main message of learning to "speak for the trees" (when they cannot speak for themselves) can be applied to the work of student affairs professionals and social justice work within student affairs. I read *The Lorax* to my students (in 2012 a movie version of the book came out, and my students and I went to the movie together—it is now available on DVD), and then we discussed the message of the work and how it can be applied to student affairs and, more explicitly, the social justice work inherent in student affairs.

The discussion usually starts with the obvious environmental message and application and moves to the idea of speaking up for others or "speaking for the trees." We then talk about when it is and is not appropriate to speak for others, and the idea behind "speaking for the trees" becomes *advocacy for* versus a *literal speaking for* another who could speak for himself or herself. We then list all of the "trees" that the student affairs profession "speaks for." The list is long, surprisingly long—long enough to cover one large blackboard and move to another.

When we start listing trees, students often start with women, African American students, Latino/a students—the simple race and gender answer. We then move on to more complex answers or "trees," and students list, for example, GLBTQ students, students with disabilities, students who are not Christian, atheists, and home-schooled students. Finally, the exercise becomes abstract, but perhaps more meaningful, and students list "trees" like students who self-harm, depressed students, students who do not find belonging, and students who wear masks. As we list more and more students, it becomes apparent how much oppression is possible on a college campus, and as we work to identify the possibility of oppression, it becomes disconcerting to see. Students often come to understand how important and needed social justice work is in student affairs. At the same time, there is a realization of truth in the word *empathy,* and suddenly the potential of our profession to serve in roles of advocacy materializes.

Then reality sets in—the list is so big! Students usually point out that we have an overwhelmingly impossible task on our hands. I agree and ask each student to go to the board and circle one or two "trees" that they feel passionate about "speaking for." I also circle my "trees." We then discuss how part of professional development is identifying and understanding what groups you want to work with and advocate for during your career, and realizing it is important to seek out professional development opportunities to learn how to best serve populations that are important to you. Through this exercise, students also come to understand that in their careers they will work both inside various social justice movements and, because of personal interests or the students they need to serve, outside various social justice movements as well.

Make a You

In order to create a plan for professional development, students must first understand themselves. I have a worksheet that I developed using clip art to help students visualize who they are. In the middle of the worksheet is a simple outline of a person. Inside the head is a picture of a brain with a blank callout box pointing to it. Inside the chest is a heart with a blank callout box pointing to it. Around the body is a box that contains a devil and an angel symbol, with room to write in; a blank box labeled *explanation*; a book with a blank cover labeled *journal*; a blank crest labeled *college*; a computer with a blank screen; and a place for the student to write her or his name. I hand out these worksheets and tell the students that we are going to make a "you" that will help guide them as they plan paths for their professional development. I then instruct the students to do the following—in pencil (after all, we all need to revise ourselves from time to time):

- Write your name on the line labeled *name.*
- In the brain box, write the most important things you believe about knowledge and learning.
- On the cover of the journal, write your beliefs about journaling. Has it helped you or not helped you become a better professional? Why or why not?
- In the college crest, write your beliefs about a college education. Who should it serve? How should it serve them? And what does a college education entail?
- On the computer screen, write about the work environment in which you are most successful.

- In the heart box, explain your deepest spiritual, religious, nonreligious, humanist beliefs.
- In the angel/devil box, write what you believe about moral and ethical decision making.
- In the explanation box, write about anything that you feel needs further explanation, attempt to illustrate how different parts of you fit together, or write about common themes in the boxes.

I never collect students' *yous* or look at what the students write, but rather instruct the students to keep them to refer to at various points in their careers to guide them in planning who they become as they learn, grow, and plan for their learning and growing.

Legacy Scrapbook: Letters to Our Colleagues

In 2010, NASPA distributed a publication at its national conference titled *Legacy Scrapbook: Letters to Our Colleagues* (NASPA, 2010). The scrapbook is a series of letters from several senior student affairs leaders, researchers, and faculty to the up-and-coming generation of student affairs professionals. Each letter contains advice, thoughts, and lessons learned in the field, over the course of many extraordinary careers. I often begin classes by reading a letter and discussing it with my students. *Legacy Scrapbook: Letters to Our Colleagues* is very well received by my students, who jokingly refer to the readings as "student affairs story time." The publication assists them in envisioning the kind of practitioner they hope to be someday. It also helps students think about what they need to learn as they advance through their careers and as they make plans for their future growth and learning. Unfortunately, the scrapbook is not readily available (unless you saved one or have access to one that someone saved). However, student affairs programs could take on the project of producing a legacy scrapbook from their program—including letters from senior administrators, faculty, and key alumni from their program. Student affairs programs could also assign students to write their own letters of advice to incoming students or advice from second-year students to first-year students. Also, faculty could assign students to write a letter to their future selves, advising paths to pursue or lessons to remember.

What Do Students Think?

For two years (2011, 2012), I have saved my plans, notes, journals, and students' written assignments and asked students who were comfortable to do so to provide me with copies of their journals. Because providing me with journals was voluntary, I do not have a full set of the same data from every student. However, I do have a complete set of assignments from 14 students, over two different classes I have taught on professional development. I have learned much from my students, and, most importantly, I have learned how important it is to help students come to know themselves better, so they can in turn serve their students better and identify their future educational needs to grow as professionals.

One of the most interesting things I have learned is that many of my students were not fully confident in their academic preparation, but felt quite confident in the practical, on-the-job training. One of my male students said,

> I feel that there are some areas that I am more confident than others. I say this not because I doubt that I know it, but because there was so much information and so much to read in our classes that it seems difficult to differentiate and remember particular things. . . . As a practitioner I am more confident in the areas that my assistantship, housing, has prepared me for. (Sam's[1] journal, 2011)

Another student echoed Sam's statement by saying,

> Some days I actually feel like I am actually becoming a "master" in my area of study and could apply all the things I have learned in the last year and a half to an actual situation and come out a better professional. Then there are times when I feel like I have sank back to the slums of middle school and I just made it out alive. . . . Theory and practice are meant to complement each other. Am I comfortable doing this? No, not yet, there have been situations where I couldn't remember the exact steps to this or that theory and it upsets me. I feel more confident in what I do, than what I know. (Rachel's journal, 2011)

Many of the students who provided me their journals expressed similar sentiments when I asked them to write about how confident they were in what they knew. This particular journal entry sparked a wonderful class discussion that set up the need for lifelong learning, understanding what you do and do not know, and continually planning for professional development. This discussion was so fruitful to set up the course that I wrote on my class plan in all capital letters, "DO THIS JOURNAL NEXT YEAR AND DISCUSS!!!" The following year, the journal and discussion revealed many of the same thoughts from students. These experiences have cemented in me the need to teach professional development.

At one point or another, all of my students shared in a paper or journal how important it is to learn about yourself in order to help others. One student said,

> Through taking Capstone this semester, I have learned that it is just as important to consider the impact that my actions, beliefs, morals, and ethics have on the organization I am working with and advising. The relationship and impact that I have on the organization and the organization has on me are aspects that I never really thought of before this course. I now understand the importance of considering how what I do [may] impact others. In order to help other people, especially students, it is vital to first understand yourself and those differences among people [that] exist. (Carrie's praxis paper, 2012)

Another student talked about learning that he was a very goal-oriented person who would see the solution to a student's problems and work "to get to that goal as quickly as possible" (Steve's praxis paper, 2011). He then went on to say that the course helped him understand that "my job is to make the student the best person that they want to be, and not to make them into the person that I want them to be" (Steve's praxis paper, 2011).

It is also clear to me that reflection became an important skill that several students found to be a valuable tool. One student wrote,

> I think professionally I will need to continue to set aside time to reflect weekly, if not daily, about what has occurred. Reflection appears to be beneficial for me even if it comes to hard realization of what is going on. I think instituting this into my workweek or when I get home from work will allow me to develop in areas that are needed. (John's praxis paper, 2011)

Another said,

> I think as a new student affairs professional it will be important for me to keep a reflective journal to watch my growth as a professional. I think it will be both helpful and interesting to see how my ethics, values, and morals develop throughout my career. Self-reflection is a great way to hold myself accountable and to evaluate myself to see if my espoused theories match my theories in action. (Kay's praxis paper, 2012)

A third student said,

> First, I must continue to write reflectively. Reflecting on my memories and journals brought new ideas and insights that I never considered in my first year, so I look forward to understanding more about how this can further impact me in a positive manner. By keeping these journals instead of

destroying them like I use[d] to do, I will be able to continue to gain understanding as I mature and develop professionally and personally. (Lauren's praxis paper, 2012)

Finally, a fourth student said, "Through structured reflection, conversation with colleagues, and periodic journaling, I hope to become a more self-aware individual who is comfortable with ambiguity" (Hank's praxis paper, 2012). This student also decided that journaling was so useful he would like to try to implement it with his next student staff.

Unless

Unless faculty take the time to help students reflect and teach them various ways to learn the skill of reflection, our students may not take the time or make the effort to get to know themselves, what skills they want to improve on, or how to achieve the goals that they have set for themselves. We need to assist our students in understanding and critiquing themselves. So when they do not know enough, are not ready for the ever-changing field of higher education, or find themselves in jobs that expect more than they can deliver, they can develop plans for their own professional development. Teaching reflection skills is one way that we as faculty can care an awful lot about our students, our field, and the future of both.

Note

1. All student names used are pseudonyms.

References

American College Personnel Association. (2006). *Statement of ethical principles and standards.* Retrieved from http://www2.myacpa.org/ethics/statement.php

Argyris, C., & Schön, D. A. (1974). *Theory in practice: Increasing professional effectiveness.* San Francisco, CA: Jossey-Bass.

Brint, S. (1993). Eliot Friedson's contribution to the sociology of professions. *Work & Occupations, 20*(3), 259–279.

Carpenter, S., & Stimpson, M. T. (2007). Professionalism, scholarly practice, and professional development in student affairs. *NASPA Journal, 44*(2), 265–284.

Coelho, P. (2006). *The alchemist.* New York: HarperCollins.

Dr. Seuss. (1971). *The lorax.* New York: Random House Books for Young Readers.

Friedson, E. (1986). *Professional powers.* Chicago, IL: University of Chicago Press.

Mitchell, R. L. (1999). *Fables, labels, and folding tables: Reflections on the student affairs profession.* Madison, WI: Atwood.

Mitchell, R. L. (2001). *Listen very loud: Paying attention in the student affairs profession.* Madison, WI: Atwood.

National Association of Student Personnel Administrators. (1990). *Standards of professional practice.* Retrieved from http://www.naspa.org/about/standards.cfm

National Association of Student Personnel Administrators. (2010). *Legacy scrapbook: Letters to our colleagues.* Retrieved from www.naspa.org/files/legacy.pdf

Ortlipp, M. (2008). Keeping and using reflective journals in the qualitative research process. *The Qualitative Report, 13*(4). Retrieved from http://www.nova.edu/ssss/QR/QR13-4/ortlipp.pdf

Pavalko, R. M. (1971). *Sociology of occupations and professions.* Itasca, IL: F. E. Peacock.

Schreiber, P. J., Dunkel, N., & Jahr, P. K. (1994). Competency based developmental programs. *The College Student Affairs Journal, 14*(1), 23–30.

St. John, E. P. (2009). *College organization and professional development: Integrating moral reasoning and reflective practice.* New York: Routledge.

9

MOVING FROM SOCIAL JUSTICE TO SOCIAL AGENCY

Keeping It Messy

Penny A. Pasque and Brittany Harris

Think of a time when you heard someone use words or act in a way that was oppressive regarding race, ethnicity, gender, class, sexual orientation, age, dis/ability, nationality, or another social identity. Yes—really—we are talking to you, the reader. Do you have a situation in your mind? What was it? How did it make you feel emotionally? Physically? Was the thing said/done about you or someone else? What did you do in the moment? What did the people around you do? About an hour later did you think, "I really wish I had said . . ."? What did you feel good about in terms of your response?

Recognizing social injustice versus acting on that injustice are two different, albeit related, things. We have both wished we had handled something differently at various points in our lifetimes. Penny worked in student and academic affairs for 10 years after earning her master's and before starting her doctoral degree and becoming a higher education and student affairs faculty member. Brittany was a master's student concentrating in student affairs with a graduate assistant position in a multicultural scholars program as we started writing this chapter. Now, as a graduate, Brittany has started the next stage of her life as the education and outreach coordinator for the Penn Women's Center at The University of Pennsylvania. Throughout our careers, we have seen oppressive comments, actions, policies, and procedures happen every day on our college campuses, and it's *not* okay. Simultaneously, colleges and universities are places of learning and growth; we cannot know what we do not know, so we must continue to teach and learn. Because of this, we argue that campuses need to foster environments that encourage learning so we may move from

The authors would like to thank Patrick Miller for reading and listening to earlier versions of this chapter.

133

understanding notions of social justice to acting as social agents for change as we (students, administrators, staff, and faculty) directly address issues of inequity, discrimination, and oppression.

The term *social justice* is used in higher education and student affairs, but often not defined. We appreciate Lee Anne Bell's (2010) definition, because she talks about social justice as both a process and a goal. She states,

> The goal of social justice is full and equal participation of all groups in a society that is mutually shaped to meet their needs. Social justice includes a vision of society in which the distribution of resources is equitable and all members are physically and psychologically safe and secure. We envision a society in which individuals are both self-determining (able to develop their full capacities) and interdependent (capable of interacting democratically with others). Social justice involves social actors who have a sense of their own agency as well as a sense of social responsibility toward and with others, their society, and the broader world in which we live. These are conditions we wish not only for our own society but also for every society in our interdependent global community. (p. 21)

The American College Personnel Association's (ACPA) *Statement of Ethical Principles and Standards* (2006) echoes this sense of agency and states, "Student affairs professionals . . . have a responsibility to contribute to the improvement of the communities in which they live and work and to act as advocates for social justice for members of those communities" (p. 5).

Although many of us may have good intentions around issues of social justice, we ask you—and ourselves—*do we always act as advocates and agents of change in front of and behind closed doors?* Do we take the knowledge we have gained through research, theories, and personal experiences and put it into practice as we act as agents of social change on a daily basis?

This chapter discusses the transition of individuals from aligning with a group, cause, or reading for a class that is "socially just" to acting as social agents as reflected in the ethical standards for the field. First, we talk about why this shift is imperative for the field. Next, we share the "three Ds," *dialogue, disregard,* and *dissonance,* as they relate to interactions among people in the field. Finally, we offer case studies that connect in-class and out-of-class experiences in the field as well as a few discussion questions in hopes that they will be useful as we interrogate the complexities of moving from thinking about social justice to acting as social agents of change through our own spheres of influence.

Why Social Agency in Higher Education and Student Affairs?

Why is acting as a social agent around issues of social justice important for the field of higher education and student affairs? Oppression across race, ethnicity, class, gender, sexual orientation, religion, ability, age, nationality, size, and additional social identities—and the intersections of these identities—continue to exist in our institutions and society at large. For example, students walking into a classroom laboratory at Central Michigan University found four nooses hanging from the gas lines in the ceiling—later determined to be deliberately placed by a 28-year-old male engineering student and declared a "racist act" by Michigan State Senator Hansen Clark (CNN, 2007; Defaultuser, 2008; Monacelli, 2007). Rutgers University first-year student Tyler Clementi committed suicide in September 2010 after his roommate Dharun Ravi used a webcam intentionally placed in his residence hall room to view and post online Tyler having sex with another man. Ravi was convicted for this hate crime and, after sentencing, apologized (New Jersey v. Dharun Ravi, 2012). In another example, George Huguely was convicted of killing ex-girlfriend Yeardley Love, a University of Virginia lacrosse student-athlete, in a domestic violence attack in the University Corner district in Charlottesville, Virginia, after drinking heavily (Commonwealth of Virginia v. George W. Huguely, V., 2012). Two years previously, Huguely had been arrested for public drunkenness and resisting arrest outside the Phi Kappa Sigma fraternity house at Washington and Lee University, where police had to tase him to subdue him.

These incidents connect issues of gender, race, ethnicity, sexual orientation, and class—to name a few. Each of these incidents is also ensconced with issues of power, privilege, oppression, violence, perceptions of masculinity, fear, crisis, public shame, intimidation, threats, residence life, Greek life, athletics, classrooms, technology, alcohol, and myriad other issues all too familiar to practitioners and scholars in the field of student affairs. Further, each of the three cases is embedded with the complexities of murder, suicide, and death of college students (for more information, see *College Student Death* by Cintron, Weathers, and Garlough, 2007).

The incidents operate at pervasive levels across individuals, institutions, and society during a time when our campuses are becoming increasingly diverse (Rhu, 2010). For example, one to two million additional young adults will seek access to higher education, and a large proportion of potential students will be students of color from low-income families (Carnevale & Fry, 2001). This group of students wants access to higher education and will continue to face inequities because of the social context in which they live (Carnevale & Fry, 2001). In terms of gender, the percentage of degrees conferred to women has increased over the years (Ropers-Huilman, 2002), yet a gap remains in terms of the disparities across institution type and degree program (Allan, 2011; Pasque & Errington Nicholson, 2011). Further, Millennial students of color; multiracial students; and lesbian, gay, bisexual, and transgender students (LGBT) in our institutions have similarities to and differences from majority students that are important for student affairs professionals to understand. Drs. Fred Bonner, Aretha Marbley, Mary Howard-Hamilton (2011), and colleagues discuss the complexities of these similarities and differences in *Diverse Millennial Students in College: Implications for Faculty and Student Affairs.*

With the increase in diversity across college campuses, the continuation of blatant hate crimes and murders, and subtle exclusionary and silencing tactics (which we discuss in what follows), we argue that institutions—and individuals within institutions—cannot continue to operate from the same dominant paradigms that have perpetuated oppression for centuries. Change is needed, and students, faculty, staff, and administrators are in a position to help make such a change. We take cues from Reason and Davis (2005) when they state,

> Ultimately the development of social justice allies must result in action that upsets the status quo—the dominant ideology and culture that maintains social inequality (Bergerson, 2003; Goodman, 2001). The status quo can be maintained consciously through active reinforcement as well as unconsciously through a lack of action. Failure to take action that upsets the status quo therefore maintains the dominant ideology. Thus, the development of social justice allies must focus on the translation of attitudes into action if anything is to change. (p. 7)

Reason and Davis specifically address "allies" who are people with agent identities—people in groups that have unearned privilege (e.g., with gender, agents would be men)—who take action to create spaces of inclusion. Social change and agency are also important for people with target identities—people in groups that have been disenfranchised, exploited, and systemically oppressed (e.g., with gender, this would be women and transgender people). For more information on social categories, classifications, and structural inequalities, see Kirk and Okazawa-Rey (2010).

Reason and Davis (2005) also stress the importance of recognizing the conscious and unconscious as we translate attitudes into action. As such, we challenge you—and ourselves—to examine what oppression and discriminatory acts on college campuses are conscious and easy to see *in addition to* what may be currently unconscious, difficult to identify, or identified and articulated by our peers.

The Three *D*s: Dialogue, Disregard, and Dissonance

The two of us have spent many hours over the past year discussing the content for this chapter, the complexities of our own social identities, social in/justices we have experienced in student affairs graduate programs and in various college environments, numerous readings and research related to these topics, hopes for practitioners in the field of student affairs, and what we want to say to you, the reader, that might potentially be beneficial. Our conversations have been fun, difficult, and emotional. As we described our experiences to each other, tears were shed, arms were flying through the air for emphasis, and we may have even slammed a hand on the table once or twice to stress a point. Our conversations were definitely "messy" as we waded through different topics and described experiences that were difficult to grasp and unpack. Even though it was messy, it felt good to come to a place of understanding and acceptance as we explored the complexities of the issues in our lives.

We have identified the concepts of dialogue, disregard, and dissonance as important to our conversation about agency and to the case studies and discussion questions that we offer at the end of the chapter. We discuss briefly in the three *D*s in the sections that follow.

Dialogue and Disregard

Penny's (2010) research shows that if you do not conform to the dominant discourse in higher education dialogues, then your ideas may be disregarded and relegated to the margins of the conversation. Specifically, your voice gets silenced either by being skipped over by facilitators or by not appearing in final reports. This sense of disregard happens to people of color, women, and community partners to institutions—no matter what the topic. In addition, this disregard happens when anyone, including people of target *and* agent identities, talks about moving from social justice to a place of action, advocacy, and social change. So, imagine that you are (or maybe you really are) a Latina graduate student with a voice of advocacy working to make change in higher education in a way that disrupts the status quo; you will be disregarded in a quadruple manner according to this study!

We have noticed that one way to disregard and silence perspectives of (a) people from target identities or (b) people with ideas that are not in the majority, whether from target or agent identities, is by asking people to conform to "civil" discussion and to display "civility" when engaged in difficult dialogues on campus. This problematic request may be a bit more of an "unconscious" issue for some readers, so stick with us while we make this point and see what you think for yourself.

For example, in their chapter "Incivility on College Campuses," Paterson and Kibler (2008) define *incivility* as negative behavior, including violence, hazing, student protest, and celebratory riots. They argue that "if higher education has a role in developing the values of a younger generation, then higher education needs to address incivility and provide direction to assist this generation of college students in becoming useful citizens" (p. 178). In another example, Joshua Hayden (2010), in "Developing Civility at the Deepest Levels of Difference," defines a civility framework as building "teamwork skills based on common agreement and accountability" (p. 23). In a third, wide-reaching example, ACPA's 2012 convention planning team came up with the theme "Create Possibilities," with three critical issues for exploration, growth, achievement, and preparation for life's work. The third of these issues is "civility on campus," including addressing violence in face-to-face and virtual communities (ACPA, 2012, para. 7). We agree with these authors that violence and hazing are not acceptable and need to be addressed, as indicated in the contemporary examples of oppression on college campuses previously mentioned. We also support various notions of teamwork. However, forms of student protest have been found to support democratic aims, student development, and digital age democracy (Biddix, Somers, & Polman, 2009). Further, we argue that common agreement may not necessarily be the desired goal, because it often asks people to conform through mediation and give up some aspects of self or of the argument for the sake of the larger group. In this way, some conceptualizations of civility argue more for the "melting pot" idea of diversity, where all elements in the pot melt and fuse together (i.e., assimilation), versus the "mosaic" concept, where people maintain unique identities and also become a rich part of the diverse and larger whole. In addition, accountability in higher education can often serve as a (self-) surveillance technique of control within the current era of conservative modernization and academic capitalism (Gildersleeve, Kuntz, Pasque, & Carducci, 2010); people in power get us to monitor each other in terms of conformity and, therefore, not question the roots of power and oppression.

The words *civility* and *incivility* also suggest a binary. We ask: Are issues and actions around social justice on campus always so binary? Are attitudes and actions so easily demarcated as "good" versus "evil," where "civility" is good and "incivility" is evil? Who determines such "good" values? What should be agreed upon in terms of civility, and by whom? And what is "useful" for "citizens" on campus (and our hope is that this term *citizen* from Paterson and Kibler [2008] includes the undocumented and international students on our campuses as full members of our communities)?

Let's break down this concept a bit further with another example: Were you "Team Jacob" or "Team Edward" if you read the *Twilight* (Meyers, 2005) books or watched the movies? The characters, and behaviors of these characters, were complex, because they connected numerous issues across race, ethnicity, nationality, class, gender, sexual orientation, indigenous culture, postcolonialism, and more. Neither Jacob nor Edward necessarily embodied pure good or pure evil, yet Twilighters (not limited to tweens) created a false dichotomy, as though one had to choose which man to celebrate and which to reject.

We see *civility* in a similar manner—the labeling of certain language or nonverbal behavior as "civil" limits the parameters of verbal and nonverbal behavior to dominant paradigms and perspectives originally defined by people with agent identities. It is used to regulate discourse. We use our own selves as examples in this instance. When in a heated conversation, Penny's arms and hands will probably become expressive as she talks; they will flail around in a descriptive manner, and she is often asked if she knows American Sign Language because of this nonverbal behavior. Penny also comes from a family (half Sicilian and half Italian) that yells, so the raising of voices is not uncommon, nor is it taken as a personal attack. When Brittany is in a heated conversation, she often gets categorized as the "angry Black woman—ABW," if her voice is even just mildly raised about a controversial issue—particularly around the topic of race. If Brittany's hair, which is natural, is in curly coils or straightened with a flat iron on that day, then she is perceived differently, based on her appearance. And, what if one of us sheds a few tears? This verbal and nonverbal behavior certainly does not fit within traditional "civil" dialogue, as defined by dominant culture, and may create dissonance in the listener if he or she is not familiar with these forms of animated communication, and there are professional and personal consequences to the speaker if we do not conform. It is messy.

Dalia Rodriguez (2011) points out, "Silence and silencing are gendered, raced and classed. People of color are often silenced by the dominant majority who maintain racial hegemony" (p. 112). As a strategy for survival, people of color have developed what W. E. B. Du Bois (1903) terms *double consciousness,* where one needs to understand the perspective of both agents and targets. "Masks of survival," or masking inner selves to not show inner feelings, has also been a way to defend against racist educational institutions and serve as a means of self-protection (Montoya, 2000; Rodriguez, 2011). Agents are only required to understand the perspective of agents; understanding of people in various target identities across race, ethnicity, nationality, class, ability, sexual orientation, and so on is optional. Yet, we have heard White people say, "I don't want you to wear a mask" as a way to try to include student affairs colleagues of color in the dialogue. But, is that invitation genuine and realistic? Can Brittany really drop the mask if her current behavior is already defined as an ABW, even though anger is a legitimate response to marginalization (Linder & Rodriguez, 2012)? Or, will this be identified as a form of "incivility," where she will be disregarded and silenced in the conversation?

Will the listener invite the mask to be dropped but then feel a sense of dissonance or uneasiness if the mask is truly dropped?

Again, we ask, whose *civility* are we talking about when we use this word? By using *civility* as an organizing rule, we automatically exclude comments and voices from public view that fall outside dominant notions of civility. Notably, can there even be dissention to the word, because who would argue against civility and for incivility? Asked another way, whom are we un/consciously including or excluding through what we may perceive as benign language?

Our colleague Karen Myers (2010) asks us *not* to think about inclusion, but to consider "Have you excluded anyone today?" (p. 16). We ask you—and ourselves—whom have you/I excluded through your/my verbal and nonverbal behavior? And, to embrace what we may define as "messy" and uncomfortable in dialogue in order to truly engage with people different from ourselves so we may move from understanding notions of social justice to working as agents of social change.

Dialogue and Dissonance

In an effort to actively encourage inclusion, we argue for expanded notions of dialogue not limited to dominant conceptualizations of civility. We understand that this might make some people experience dissonance or feel uncomfortable. Other people may feel extremely comfortable in this expanded and inclusive notion of dialogue. For this reason, if you experience dissonance when talking and acting around issues of social justice, then we say to you—great! This means you are pushing on your own "learning edge" or "getting messy."

As Pat Griffin (1997) points out, the boundaries of our comfort zones are our learning edges. When we find ourselves at the limit of our comfort zones, we are in the best place to expand our understandings, take in different perspectives, and broaden our awareness. Learning edges are often signaled by feelings of annoyance, anger, anxiety, surprise, confusion, or defensiveness. This feeling of—what we call—*dissonance* may happen when members of your group are not conforming to notions of "civil discourse." It may happen when a student in your class becomes what you may label as an ABW, flails arms around, cries in class, or is completely silent.

When you are feeling dissonance, it is important to figure out why, learn from it, and push on your own learning edge. We also think it is important to do this without falling off the edge! If you fall off the edge, then you stop engaging in the dialogue, learning from the conversation, and moving toward action. For example, Penny has seen this in her Diversity in Higher Education course, when students mentally "check out" or stay silent as they think through a difficult discussion around their target or agent identities.

This can be a place of perceived safety. Yet, if you continue to stay in this "checked-out" space and "spin" in your head on an issue, then you have the potential to remain stagnant. Consider, what is it that you are spinning on? The dominant messages told to us in society or by role models in your life? A new conceptualization of the issue? A comment made by a peer in your class? What are the implications for you to continue to "spin" in this place and not explore the complexity of the issue and learn from it? What are the implications if you "spin" on a place of fear and dissonance without working with your support systems to figure out how to unpack the issues? Who will benefit/suffer if you engage in dialogue with the group; people from target or agent identities?

We certainly do not want you to fall off the edge, and, as Linder and Rodriguez (2012) found, it is important to provide safe spaces and programs for activists to explore their multiple identities and understandings about systems of power and privilege. We also do not want to confuse safety with comfort (Griffin & Ouellett, 1997). Dissonance can be a good thing, because learning is not always comfortable within a safe environment. We ask you—and ourselves—to stay "checked in" and engage in the dialogue or step out; process with a peer, counselor, or facilitator; and then reengage next time the group is together. In this way, pushing on this learning edge may help us to understand issues of social justice in a different way and figure out what this means as you move toward social agency.

On a related note, Harro offers the cycles of socialization (2000b) and liberation (2000a), which are useful when exploring dissonance and how to move to a sense of agency. The cycle of socialization process within a culture is "*pervasive* (coming from all sides and sources), *consistent* (patterned and predictable), *circular* (self-supporting), *self-perpetuating* (intra-dependent) and often *invisible* (unconscious and unmanned)" (2000b, p. 15). Because of this, dominant perspectives are reinforced through institutional and cultural messages, which results in dissonance, silence, collusion, ignorance, violence, and internalized patterns of power. At this point, we have a choice to reflect on our own socialization process and do nothing—and thereby perpetuate the status quo—or make change by raising consciousness, interrupting patterns, educating ourselves and others, and taking action in various ways.

Harro's (2000a) cycle of liberation regarding individual, collaborative, community, and culture change requires

> a struggle against discrimination based on race, class, gender, sexual identity, ableism and age—those barriers that keep large portions of the population from having access to economic and social justice, from being able to participate fully in the decisions affecting our lives, from having a full share of both the rights and responsibilities of living in a free society. (p. 450)

Such liberatory and emancipatory perspectives may happen as you engage in dialogue, experience dissonance, then choose to interrupt dominant paradigms of oppression through your work in higher education and student affairs. These changes may be done in front of or behind closed doors through individual actions and institutional programs, policies, and procedures. We encourage you to explore these cycles, if you have not done so already. There are additional models for dialogue and change that may be useful, such as the intergroup dialogue programs at institutions across the country, which are described in *Facilitating Intergroup Dialogues: Bridging Differences, Catalyzing Change* (Maxwell, Nagda, & Thompson, 2011).

Case Studies

We ask you, and we ask ourselves, How do we take the conversations about social justice in classrooms and professional development workshops to a place of action in the field? How do we use what we have learned in dialogue with each other and transfer it to our work in a way that moves us from teaching and learning about the importance of social justice to actually engaging as social agents of change? We offer the following case studies as a way for you to consider different scenarios, engage in dialogue, and explore your own answers to these questions.

The case studies and discussion questions focus on student affairs graduate students in the classroom and new professionals outside the classroom. They also move from more dualistic thinking to multiple perspectives. We used Broido's Model of College Student Ally Development (Broido, 2000; Broido & Reason, 2005) as we developed the case studies.

Case Study One: Faculty and Students in the Classroom

It is the 35th hour that I have spent in the Diversity in Higher Education graduate course with 19 of my peers and Dr. Pasque. The discussions have been pretty intense. So far, we have explored social identity, personal narratives around identity, theories of oppression and privilege, the cycle of liberation and oppression, and numerous other topics that have helped to give me some language to give to things that I was thinking about. We have also engaged in a number of different experiential learning activities, including the culture box, who is here?, privilege walk, caucus groups, and fishbowls. Today the exercise is called "cross the line." Dr. Pasque reads a statement about the readings, movies, and discussions from throughout the semester. After hearing the statement, I have to stand on the "yes" side of the room or "cross the line" and stand on the "no" side of the room. After we choose a side, we discuss why we are on the side of the room that we chose. Sometimes I agree with people who are on the same side as me, and sometimes I don't, which is odd, because we both chose to move to the same side of the line. This definitely shows me that I can agree with people by saying "yes" to something, but I may agree for a very different reason than they agree with it.

There was one point in the discussion that I felt pretty surprised with my own response. About halfway through the list, Dr. Pasque said, "Race and ethnicity should be taken into consideration in college admissions processes, yes or no?" I picked "yes" and talked about how I think people have not had the same educational experience in school or at home before getting to college. I also said that if there was an equal playing field, then we would not have to take race into consideration; however, at this point, we should take it into account. Some people agreed with me, and some disagreed. It was a really deep discussion.

Next, Dr. Pasque asked, "I support affirmative action, yes or no?" This is where I was so surprised! I switched sides and moved to the "no" side, because I have never supported affirmative action. A lot of people switched sides from "yes" to "no," or vice versa. I switched sides because, for me, I don't want someone to think that I got into college because I'm Chickasaw and because of affirmative action. I want people to think that I deserve to be here just like everyone else. We discussed the complexities of the issue and of the power of language. We also talked about how affirmative action policies are often not understood completely—I have to say that I didn't really understand it. From what I understand, now that we had the discussion, it means that people do have to meet the standards of the institution and then, when there are too many qualified applicants, admissions officers must decide who should be admitted to the college, who should be wait-listed, and who should be denied. At this point in time, admissions no longer awards people "points," but they consider the applicant in a holistic way. They consider if the student was a leader, is a legacy, is a student of color, did community service, grew up in an urban or rural environment, and a number of other factors. I think the term *affirmative action* is not really understood, and people make assumptions that someone does not deserve to be at the institution because of the color of their skin.

Dr. Pasque then asked, "What about gender?" "What about class?" "What about learning, physical, or psychological dis/abilities?" We all pretty much stayed on the same side of the line if the question was about race, ethnicity, gender, or class. But, when we got to various abilities, then people switched sides, talked about the Americans with Disabilities Act, the shootings on college campuses, and the conversation continued to get messy!

Case Study One: Discussion Questions

- What happened in this class?
- Why do you think some students switched sides after hearing the term *affirmative action*? What if the person who switched sides was from a target identity? An agent identity?
- How does language impact social constructions of race, ethnicity, gender, class, sexual orientation, religion, ability, and other social identities?
- What is your definition of affirmative action? What is your institution's definition? What is the legal definition of affirmative action? What physical reactions do you have to the term *affirmative action*, if any?
- What is the responsibility of institutions to recruit and provide support services for students with varying abilities? What is the value in hiring a staff that is reflective of students in terms of race, gender, sexual orientation, nationality, ability, and so on?
- What can you do in front of and behind closed doors (e.g., designing programs, developing policies, determining hiring practices, hiring student staff, selecting grant recipients) to support students of color in a way that moves from the cycle of socialization to the cycle of liberation? Women and transgender students? Students with varying abilities?
- What can you do in front of and behind closed doors (e.g., recruiting, hiring, sustaining, and daily practices) to support administrators of color in a way that moves from the cycle of socialization to the cycle of liberation? Women and transgender administrators? Administrators with varying abilities?

Case Study Two: Students Outside the Classroom

Ghetto, loud, uneducated, bossy, nagging, complaining, needy, nigger. I could not believe that he just used all these words to describe me as a Black woman. *Intelligent, kind, resourceful, opinionated,* and *determined* sound like a better fit for me. The person on the other side of the table at the restaurant after our student development theories class is not a bigot who wanted to cut me down. He is Black and a "friend" who wanted me to know how he felt about most Black women. This is completely shocking to me that he could share these thoughts with me so freely and think that I would not be hurt or offended by them. As he realizes his remarks cut me deeply he says, "But you are the exception." Out of shock and frustration, I laugh and try to help him understand that I am not the exception out of millions of Black women and how hurtful it is to hear him say such degrading things about us.

I think about my mother, grandmother, and a host of friends and family, all Black women who have impacted my life. I think about their strength, dedication, and perseverance in a world where often they finish last. I think about my friend's mother, who is Black, and how she might feel about the harsh comments her son just made about her and her counterparts. I hurt for him, myself, and hurt at knowing these and similar conversations are happening on college campuses across the country.

As I explain why these accusations aren't true and are very hurtful, I see that, although he was engaged in this conversation, he is now starting to disengage. He does not want to hear what I have to say, because he has already made up in his mind about what he thinks about Black women. And, of course he shares this with me after class and not in our class, so I don't have my friends to back me up. I have some choices at this point. I can throw on my "angry Black woman" cape and become an example of what he thinks all Black women are. I can show him through my daily example why his claims are off base. Or, I can do a little of both. Why is he putting me in the position to have to make this choice?

Case Study Two: Discussion Questions

- What happened at this restaurant after class? What might you do in a similar situation?
- Is Brittany's friend being "civil" in this conversation? Is she? How do you define "civility" and "incivility"?
- Is it Brittany's responsibility to say something? Nothing? What is her role as an agent of social change in this case? Is it different talking about difficult issues with friends versus family versus colleagues? If so, why? If not, why not?
- What are some "hurt words" that you have experienced? What are some hurt words you have heard used in class or on campus? What do you do in these situations? What are the various strategies or ways you might address hurt words?
- Lee Anne Bell (1997) describes internalized oppression and states, "Oppressive beliefs are internalized by victims as well as perpetrators. The

idea that poor people somehow deserve and are responsible for poverty, rather than the economic system that structures and requires it, is learned by poor and affluent alike. Homophobia, the deep fear and hatred of homosexuality, is internalized by both straight and gay people. Jews as well as Gentiles absorb antisemitic stereotypes" (p. 4). In what ways does internalized oppression show up in this case study? In your own personal or professional life?

- What action can you take if someone starts to "check out" of the conversation? What action can you take if you notice yourself "checking out"?

- Is it always on the person with the target identity (woman) to be responsible to educate the person with the agent identity (man)? How can people in target identities pick and choose when to educate and when to walk away? How can people in agent identities take action to educate themselves on an ongoing basis?

Case Study Three: In the Profession

I'm so frustrated with the university's policy change! I'm the codirector of a small social justice residential program that has been going well. My boss just told me and my codirector that the nameless, faceless "university" just changed the budget. Instead of employee health benefits coming from the general department fund, they will now be coming from our small program budget. The program will be allocated money to cover this change; however, if a staff member goes over their allotment, then we will have to deduct the money from somewhere else. If a staff member does not use all their allotment, then we will get to spend this money, or the department will take it back at the end of the year.

The codirector and I met with the administrative assistant who is in charge of budget operations to discuss the new policy and the specific procedures that accompany this change. At one point, the codirector says to the administrative assistant, "You need to watch Jeffrey's health expenditures." Yikes! I could not believe that he said that—to watch Jeffrey's expenditures and not the other four administrators in the program!!! I guarantee he said that because Jeffrey, a gay man of color, has told us that he has HIV. This is not okay. I'm so mad but really try to hold in my anger. I say—in what I really hope is a fairly factual and calm voice—"I think we need to watch everyone's expenditures or none of our expenditures." I can see he got the point. He just said, "Yeah—okay," and then we move on. Do I bring this up when we are together without our administrative assistant, or just let it go? This job as a codirector is far messier than I ever imagined!

Case Study Three: Discussion Questions

- What happened behind closed doors in this programmatic budget meeting?
- What would happen if the codirector did not say anything and the administrative assistant monitored only one staff member's health care expenditures? Was the administrative assistant in any position to mention any injustice if she or he noticed it?
- What are the implications of a codirector confronting another codirector in front of a supervisee? Could the codirector who wanted to watch Jeffrey's expenditures have brought this up to the other codirector prior to their talking with the administrative assistant? Could the codirector who was angry have waited for another time to say that this was not okay? Should they discuss this later on in a follow-up conversation where it is only the two of them? What are the pros and cons of each situation?
- What would you say in this moment? What might be said in a follow-up conversation with the codirector? With the administrative assistant?
- Is there any conversation about this—or any related topic—to be had with Jeffrey? Why or why not?
- If you were the codirector, what might you watch for/be alerted to if you were a part of this conversation?
- Who is (or who are) the "nameless, faceless university" administrators in this scenario? At your institution? What are the complexities of being employed as a codirector by the university and using this language?
- How might this new budget policy impact future recruitment and hiring decisions in conscious or unconscious ways?
- Is this an example of moving from social justice to social agency behind closed doors? Why or why not?
- What are the student development theories that might relate to this case study?
- In what ways may exercises presented (in this chapter or elsewhere) or student development theories be reductive?
- In what ways may exercises or theories be useful?
- How do theories of social justice show up in your work in the field?

Conclusion

Carol Gilligan (2011) talks about the importance of action, connection, resistance, and the political. We share it with you in the hopes that it inspires you to action, as it did for us:

> Voices from the underground, speaking under the sign of repression, marking dissociations that are still tenuous, knowledge that is fragile, reaching out for connections that sustain the hope that a secret underground will become a public resistance. Then a healthy resistance, rather than turning inward and becoming corrosive, can stay in the open air of relationships. And by remaining political, work to bring a new order of living into the world. (p. 163)

We encourage you—not to turn corrosively inward—but to take the knowledge from your experiences, dialogues with your colleagues, readings and theories in the field, and case studies offered, and move from a place of understanding social justice to social agency in order to work toward social change on a daily basis. The status quo is not okay, and we all (including ourselves) need to engage in lifelong learning on social justice and social agency.

Finally, I, Brittany, would like to leave you with some thoughts. Some of the best classes and greatest transformative experiences in student affairs occurred when I took off my security blanket and dug deeply into difficult dialogues. I believe it is my duty to do my best to ignite powerful and transformative discussions about issues of race, class, gender, ability, religion, and sexual orientation both in and out of the classroom. So many times we forget that what we have learned in our classes not only gives us a theoretical framework for guiding students, but also practical application when working with students *and* our peers in front of and behind closed doors. Some of my first real discussions about my identity did not happen until my master's program. During those discussions, not only was I sharing my stories and working through my own "stuff," but I was also learning about my peers and the barriers they have faced. We learned to be allies for one another during those times, to get messy in our conversations, and to simply agree to disagree. I believe it was because of those "not-so-civil" dialogues that we were able to grow together and really become invested in each other's success, and that is the type of student affairs professional I want to be for the students I serve. I hope to foster safe, supportive, and open climates that will build the foundation for us to have our own dialogues, for if we are not practicing the art of being a true ally for our peers, how do we expect to be allies for our students and operate as true agents of change?

References

Allan, E. J. (2011). Women's status in higher education: Equity matters. *ASHE Higher Education Report, 37*(1), iii–163. San Francisco, CA: Jossey-Bass.

American College Personnel Association. (2006). *Statement of ethical principles and standards*. Washington, DC: Author. http://www2.myacpa.org/ethics/statement.php

American College Personnel Association. (2012). *Program overview*. Retrieved from http://convention.myacpa.org/louisville2012/program/

Bell, L. A. (1997). Theoretical foundations for social justice. In M. Adams, L. B. Bell, & P. Griffin (Eds.), *Teaching for diversity and social justice* (pp. 1–14). New York: Routledge.

Bell, L. A. (2010). Theoretical foundations. In M. Adams, W. J. Blumenfeld, C. Castañeda, H. W. Hackman, M. L. Peters, & X. Zúñiga (Eds.), *Readings for diversity and social justice: An anthology on racism, antisemitism, sexism, heterosexism, ableism, and classism* (2nd ed., pp. 21–26). New York: Routledge.

Biddix, J. P., Somers, P. A., & Polman, J. L. (2009). Protest reconsidered: Identifying democratic civic engagement learning outcomes. *Innovative Higher Education, 34*, 133–147.

Bonner, F. A., II, Marbley, A. F., & Howard-Hamilton, M. F. (Eds.). (2011). *Diverse millennial students in college: Implications for faculty and student affairs*. Sterling, VA: Stylus.

Broido, E. M. (2000). The development of social justice allies during college: A pheonomenological investigation. *Journal of College Student Development, 41*(1), 3–18.

Broido, E. M., & Reason, R. D. (2005). The development of social justice attitudes and actions: An overview of current understandings. *New Directions for Student Services, 110*, 17–28.

Carnevale, A. P., & Fry, R. A. (2001). *Economics, demography, and the future of higher education policy*. New York: National Governors Association.

Cintron, R., Weathers, E. T., & Garlough, K. (Eds.). (2007). *College student death: Guidance for a caring campus*. Lanham, MD: University Press of America.

CNN U.S. (2007). *Four nooses found in Central Michigan University classroom*. Retrieved from http://articles.cnn.com/2007-11-15/us/cmu.nooses_1_nooses-students-classroom?_s=PM:US

Commonwealth of Virginia v. George W. Huguely, V., 2012.

Defaultuser. (2008, August 25). *Michigan hate crime bill partial response to noose incident*. Retrieved on May 30, 2012, from http://www.cm-life.com/2008/08/25/michiganhatecrimebillpartialresponsetonooseincident/

Du Bois, W. E. B. (1903). *The souls of black folk: Essays and sketches*. New York: Bantam Classic.

Gildersleeve, E. R., Kuntz, A., Pasque, P. A., & Carducci, R. (2010). The role of critical inquiry in (re)constructing the public agenda for higher education: Confronting the conservative modernization of the academy. *The Review of Higher Education, 34*(1), 85–121.

Gilligan, C. (2011). *Joining the resistance.* Malden, MA: Polity Press.

Griffin, P. (1997). Introductory modules. In M. Adams, L. B. Bell, & P. Griffin (Eds.), *Teaching for diversity and social justice* (pp. 48–66). New York: Routledge.

Griffin, P., & Ouellett, M. L. (1997). Facilitating social justice education courses. In M. Adams, L. B. Bell, & P. Griffin (Eds.), *Teaching for diversity and social justice* (pp. 89–113). New York: Routledge.

Harro, B. (2000a). The cycle of liberation. In M. Adams, W. J. Blumenfeld, C. Castañeda, H. W. Hackman, M. L. Peters, & X. Zúñiga (Eds.), *Readings for diversity and social justice: An anthology on racism, antisemitism, sexism, heterosexism, ableism, and classism* (pp. 15–21). New York: Routledge.

Harro, B. (2000b). The cycle of socialization. In M. Adams, W. J. Blumenfeld, C. Castañeda, H. W. Hackman, M. L. Peters, & X. Zúñiga (Eds.), *Readings for diversity and social justice: An anthology on racism, antisemitism, sexism, heterosexism, ableism, and classism* (pp. 463–470). New York: Routledge.

Hayden, J. M. (2010). Developing civility at the deepest levels of difference: An alternative framework for religious pluralism on campus. *About Campus*, 19–25.

Kirk, G., & Okazawa-Rey, M. (2010). Identities and social locations: Who am I? Who are my people? In M. Adams, W. J. Blumenfeld, C. Castañeda, H. W. Hackman, M. L. Peters, & X. Zúñiga (Eds.), *Readings for diversity and social justice: An anthology on racism, antisemitism, sexism, heterosexism, ableism, and classism.* (2nd ed., pp. 8–14). New York: Routledge.

Linder, C., & Rodriguez, K. L. (2012). Learning from the experiences of self-identified women of color activists. *Journal of College Student Development, 53*(3), 383–397.

Maxwell, K. E., Nagda, B. R., & Thompson, M. C. (Eds.). (2011). *Facilitating intergroup dialogue: Bridging differences, catalyzing change.* Sterling, VA: Stylus.

Meyers, S. (2005). *Twilight: The twilight saga.* New York: Little, Brown, and Company.

Monacelli, N. (2007, November 18). *Student confesses in CMU noose case.* Retrieved from http://www.wzzm13.com/news/story.aspx?storyid=83851

Montoya, M. (2000). Silence and silencing: Their centripetal and centrifugal forces in legal communication, pedagogy and discourse. *University of Michigan Journal of Law Reform, 33*(263), 1–62.

Myers, K. A. (2010, November–December). A new vision for disability education: Moving from the add-on. *About Campus*, 15–21.

New Jersey v. Dharun Ravi, 2012.

Pasque, P. A. (2010). *American higher education, leadership, and policy: Critical issues and the public good.* New York: Palgrave Macmillan.

Pasque, P. A., & Errington Nicholson, M. (2011). Preface. In P. A. Pasque & M. Errington Nicholson (Eds.), *Empowering women in higher education and student affairs: Theory, research, narratives and practice from feminist perspectives* (pp. xv–xxi). Sterling, VA: Stylus/American College Personnel Association.

Paterson, B. G., & Kibler, W. L. (2008). Incivility on college campuses. In J. M. Lancaster & D. M. Waryold (Eds.), *Student conduct practice: The complete guide for student affairs professionals* (pp. 175–201). Sterling, VA: Stylus.

Reason, R. D., & Davis, T. L. (2005). Antecedents, precursors, and concurrent concepts in the development of social justice attitudes and actions. *New Directions for Student Services, 110,* 5–15.

Rhu, M. (2010). *Minorities in higher education: Twenty-fourth status report.* Washington, DC: American Council on Education.

Rodriguez, D. (2011). Silence as speech: Meanings of silence for students of color in predominantly White classrooms. *International Review of Qualitative Inquiry, 4*(1), 111–144.

Ropers-Huilman, R. (2002). Feminism in the academy: Overview. In A. M. M. Alemán & K. A. Renn (Eds.), *Women in higher education: An encyclopedia* (pp. 109–118). Santa Barbara, CA: ABC-CLIO.

PART FOUR

MOVING FORWARD

10

IMPLICATIONS FOR DAILY
PRACTICE AND LIFE

Kimberly A. Kline

Communication among humans is evolving quicker than we could have ever imagined. Along with rapid advances in the way that we communicate with others comes a moral and ethical responsibility to do so in a caring, just, and inclusive way. The fact of the matter is, at times we, as higher education and student affairs colleagues, (mis)use technology and mistreat each other. St. John (2009a) purports that we must come up with ways to quicken our pace of integrating moral and ethical understandings into our communication patterns in order to keep up with such changes. Though this sounds like a daunting task, it can be compared with the evolution of the printing press. Dima Blundell (2013) writes:

> The printing press by Gutenberg was a magnificent invention—it made books quicker and it allowed more people to be able to read them. It was truly an invention of the Renaissance era, and it changed life to a faster world through writing and printing. . . . It was a great invention of its' [sic] time, and it [was] most likely the most useful invention of its' [sic] time. The press changed so many things, because people could send out messages much quicker, and more people could receive those messages. . . . People used the press mostly for arguing against things, and protests went very far very quickly because of the printing press. This can be compared with the Internet, which has helped wealthy and not-so-wealthy citizens both with protests and many other things like getting a message out. Two ways that this has happened recently is with the United States Presidential election, and in war in countries like Syria. In Syria, smart phones have allowed citizens to use twitter and texting to warn about bombs or hurt people who need help. Both the printing press and the Internet are very complicated but very good inventions; both have helped life as we know it. (p. 1)

If we juxtapose Dima's thoughts with the questions that Penny and Brittany pose in Chapter 9 of this text, we may discover the first steps of how to better deal with conversations, regardless of the mode of communication:

> We ask you, and we ask ourselves, how do we take the conversations about social justice in classrooms and professional development workshops to a place of action in the field? How do we use what we have learned in dialogue with each other and transfer it to our work in a way that moves us from teaching and learning about the importance of social justice to actually engaging as social agents of change? (p. 138)

Penny and Brittany's questions are relevant for us in various roles on campus, whether we are running professional development workshops, serving as co-learners in the classroom, or coordinating a campus/departmental program.

In *Reflection in Action*, we note that, although there are large amounts of theory imparted on paraprofessionals and scholar/professionals in our field, there is a dearth of tools available to them to allow them to practice these theories. We have a moral and professional responsibility to provide safe settings, whether they are online, in person, or virtual, so emerging higher education and student affairs professionals can practice taking part in difficult conversations and situations that are described in greater detail in *Reflection in Action*. In the following sections I will attempt to summarize some implications for practice and everyday life.

Implications for Practice and Everyday Life

In "Reflecting on the Past: Shaping the Future of Student Affairs," Stebleton and Aleixo (2011) present a set of questions through which we should reflect on our professional practice: Where are we headed? What is our story? (which I have adapted to, What are our stories?) What is our hope? When can we dance? These questions are relevant to the reflection in action of our practice and serve as a way to situate the claims presented in this text.

Where Are We Headed?

Our purpose at the outset of this project was to describe ways in which graduate students in higher education and student affairs could learn to obtain a critical social understanding of current social justice, reflection, and actionable knowledge to offer new pathways for practice in a contemporary world. Lane (2011) notes, "Higher education will continue to be impacted by the changing demographics of students seeking educational opportunities as well as global, multicultural, and technological influences" (p. 9). Penny A. Pasque and Brittany Harris in Chapter 9 describe the current situation as "messy"— and purport that this state of affairs may be perpetuated by a dominant voice within higher education and student affairs professionals. For an example of this, I think of the use of Jim Collins's text *Good to Great* (2001), which many college and university presidents over the past decade have asked their faculty and staff to read. In this text, Collins describes good-to-great companies as those who create a culture of discipline, inspiring employees to work hard not through threats or hierarchy, but by hiring people who are inspired and have a strong work ethic already and by providing true incentives and creating egalitarian work environments. Good-to-great companies also used technology as an accelerator to further their success, as opposed to comparison companies, who either did not use rapidly improving technology, or relied too heavily on technology to carry their business. Good-to-great companies saw technologies as another important tool to further the same goals they had always had and were therefore successful at using technology and were not bogged down by hype (Odden, 2012). When you think about the points made in Collins's text, it is important to consider the stark contradiction between espoused values versus values in use (Argyris & Schön, 1974) by the simple act of college presidents asking their community to read this text. For example, by college and university presidents encouraging (and sometimes requiring) *Good to Great* as a reading assignment, they are espousing that faculty and staff on college campuses should be inspired not through threats or hierarchy. Yet the cold truth remains that on many college campuses, calls for accountability and transparency are being manifested through threats of downsizing and doing more with less.

Good-to-great companies also used technology creatively to further their existing successes, as opposed to overusing technology to achieve a goal. The majority of college and university campuses in the United States are currently in favor, however, of online learning wherever possible as a means of narrowing the growing financial and capital building deficits on those campuses. Yet, research regarding online learning is still emerging, with a growing narrative suggesting that blended learning works best. And finally, good-to-great companies saw technology as one tool toward supporting goals that were already present within a professional community. Because of this, I would of course advocate online learning if it better served our college-going populations. However, many times online learning via courses, programs, departments, or entire schools is implemented with little regard for the inequity that may accompany the philosophical shift.

Ed St. John makes very clear the notion of seizing responsibility within higher education in Chapter 1. We simply cannot ignore the importance of the dialogues that we have with others in physical and virtual spaces with the college-going public. It is only then that we can begin having conversations that bring about social agency through actionable change.

It is okay to not always publicly test assumptions—particularly when you are operating within an institutionalistic frame and the playing field is marginalizing toward some of the members of that community. Rather, we must work toward developing communities of practice, wherein all members agree that individual community members are more important than the issues that are being brought to the community. Some contributions from scholars expanded the current scope of social justice and multiculturalism literature to include theoretical perspectives on communicative action, social agency, critical reflection, and action research models. For example, if critical reflection is encouraged for new professionals, particularly with regard to how one's worldview is constructed, these professionals will then be equipped to facilitate similar critical consciousness in students. Reflection in action provides opportunities for newer professionals to communicate and make meaning of their practical and theoretical learning. Helping professionals develop their personal praxis or philosophy and an individual critical consciousness through action theories and reflection may empower professionals to transform institutions into caring communities that value differences as well as guide students in social justice ideas; acknowledge the role of power, privilege, and oppression; and translate intentions into actions.

What Are Our Stories?

Because the spirit of the *Reflection in Action* text lies within placing more emphasis on the growth of the individual professional or emerging professional in higher education and student affairs, I would like to share how I became interested in the topic of reflecting in action and its impact on social agency within colleges and universities.

It has been 19 years since I started reflecting on my professional practice. All of this took place after taking part in professional situations, as opposed to the notion of reflecting in action, because in 1994 it was not commonplace for a new professional in student affairs to share valid information or publicly test theories in professional settings. While pursuing my master's degree, I was consistently encouraged to speak openly about issues that took place within professional settings. To be authentic, before being authentic was avant-garde. Upon arrival in my first professional setting, I felt my voice silenced on most occasions. The biggest challenge with this was the fact that I worked a "second-shift" professional position, handling evening and weekend operations for a student union. If you can imagine, I was one of the few professional staff members present after 5:00 p.m. Yet, when issues arose—such as custodial workers whom I supervised who were paid below minimum wage (it was a right-to-work state) and were working two consecutive eight-hour shifts—my concerns, in this case for the workers' well-being, were left by the wayside. By the time I got to my second professional position, I had many more questions than answers, and I began to feel a bit jaded by the large gap between values that both of these institutions espoused and their actual values in use. At the time, I did not realize that it was okay for these situations to be "messy" and made the blind assumption that this was a typical work environment for a student affairs professional.

As time went on, I began to realize that those in power really perpetuated not so much an explicitly hostile environment—rather, those in power perpetuated cultural norms that permeated the campus environment. You could actually watch individuals proclaim to advocate for this cause or that underrepresented group, yet, some of their behavior was incredibly marginalizing, counter to what they espoused. What was more concerning to me was the fact that I began exerting those same marginalizing tendencies with others, in an effort to survive in this work culture.

Fast-forward five years, and I met Ed St. John in a professional development course. During my time in this course, we were encouraged to do things, like "Just jump in the river—it will be okay!" And told, "You have not dealt with that aspect of yourself yet." In examining some of the issues that I later grew to understand were my own issues of oppression of self, I was able to do some reflection to figure out why my worldview was constructed in the way that it was. Two of the best pieces of advice that, to this day, I have ever received came from Ed St. John. First, when a group of colleagues at a café in New Orleans asked why I was not going to apply for jobs in the Deep South, my reply was, "Because I am afraid I will be shot on the way to my car for my views on life." Ed looked at me across the table and said, "You really have to get over your prejudice of the South." He was surgically correct, and I was left with an issue to ponder for several years. I now believe that it was not so much a deep-seated prejudice against the Deep South, as it was the fact that I did not know enough about the Deep South, and so I made very unfair assumptions about that region of the United States.

The second piece of advice I received from Ed was when I continued to deconstruct and reconstruct my understandings of race and class and my privileged role in one and not the other. I could not decide whether to speak up for those who were marginalized in a situation or simply to maintain my silence. Ed offered this piece of advice: "You want to engage those with whom you philosophically disagree in dialogue so that you can move the dialogue forward in a shared way. If you do not do this, you will silence them, and they will leave the table—you need to have all of the players at the table if you want to bring about actionable change." I am so grateful for these life lessons because they really shaped the direction my research took and also gave me great opportunities for self-growth. Also, these lessons helped build my confidence, by engaging in dialogues that were not clean, where the consequences were higher, but where the greatest amount of actionable change could take place. It is important for all of us to understand what our stories are so that we can deal with issues of oppression, prejudice, and indifference to move toward dialogues that are more caring and honest in nature.

What Is Our Hope?

In 2010, the American College Personnel Association (ACPA) and the National Association of Student Personnel Administrators (NASPA) task forces coauthored a document titled "Professional Competency Areas for Student Affairs Practitioners." In it, they suggest that higher education and student affairs professionals should be able to (a) "facilitate dialogue effectively among disparate audiences," (b) "demonstrate fair treatment to all individuals and change aspects of the environment that do not promote fair treatment," and (c) "analyze the interconnectedness of societies worldwide and how these global perspectives impact institutional learning" (ACPA & NASPA, 2010, p. 12). A positive aspect of calls for accountability within higher education is that it is forcing professionals and leaders within higher education and student affairs professional organizations to examine the values and mission that guide our professional practice. In other words, we may actually be rewarded as professionals for seeking to understand ways in which the college-going public learns, develops, and serves. If we can seize this responsibility by having a voice in guiding principles of our professional organizations, it can provide a unified approach to lobbying for professional development and practice that is caring in nature.

When Can We Dance?

As authors, we propose that this text further extends the core concepts in social justice and multiculturalism in higher education and student affairs to core courses in the field of higher education and student affairs administration. Our goal was to provide an alternative lens through which to examine the intersection of social justice and agency education and professional practice in our field.

The chapters within this book explore several points regarding rapidly changing times within institutions of higher education. Within these changes there will be circumstances that challenge higher education and student affairs professionals in ways we do not yet know. One thing that will remain is the presence of student affairs professionals who continue to serve on the front line of many social changes. In Chapter 1, St. John notes, "Professionals in higher education and student affairs confront many circumstances that undermine the espoused goals related to the development of global and social consciousness as they engage in overcoming recurrent, historic patterns of conflict within educational organizations" (p. 8). I believe our profession has evolved to a point where we can no longer just "support" or "assist" with upholding the work that goes on within the higher education classroom. Rather, there is an increasing need to address the blurred line that is omnipresent in our conversations with students, staff, faculty, administrators, and stakeholders, regarding the issues of personal responsibility, difficult dialogues with those we are different from, and inequality that is becoming greater and greater in higher education. As a profession, we continue to attempt to fit opportunities for students into frames that are outdated and no longer serve the needs of the college-going public. Yet, few stakeholders in higher education, regardless of their status, are willing to take responsibility for the fairness that is sought and needed within this new paradigm of higher education on the contemporary college campus. Inequality continues to exist in financial aid policies, employment practices, enrollment standards, intentional speech, and espoused values (Coleman, 2012).

So perhaps I am proposing a new understanding, specifically for the higher education and student affairs community, that is shockingly simple. Authors have called for communicative action (Bourdieu & Passeron, 1990; Habermas, 1990; Rawls, 2001), social agency (Pasque, 2010; Pasque & Harris, Chapter 9, this text), and professional responsibility (St. John, 2009a; 2009b). Though I uphold these calls, I believe that a new approach that is counter to new frames—which, by nature of us as human reasoners, become more new frames—is necessary.

Three Paths to Understanding Others

Be Open to New Understandings: The Art of Listening

For higher education and student affairs professionals, being open to new understandings and role modeling this behavior for new professionals is essential. Instead of operating through dense frames of learning and developmental outcomes, we have to authentically be able to listen to one another. As Kate Boyle notes in Chapter 3, we have to make the individual with whom we are having the dialogue the priority, more so than the topics that we are addressing. Viewing our professional life through this alternative lens will help us to not be as overwhelmed by the modes through which we are communicating; rather, it will help us make centering on the dialogue with the other (colleague, student, supervisor, or partner) the priority.

Provide Safe Spaces and Tools for Difficult Dialogues With Love and Care

I suggest we promote the notions of love and care when providing safe spaces and tools for our students to practice having difficult dialogues with others. Gratitude is truly underrated and can be a humbling path toward understanding ourselves. The role of gratitude can have a unique role in the education of the college-going public, with boundless possibilities of how that gratitude will be applied to their communities, as they become the next community leaders. Understanding ourselves can lead to freeing ourselves of our own oppression and can have far-reaching implications regarding peace and understanding with one another. Once we forgive ourselves, we are better equipped to forgive others. A mentor of mine noted that she had beaten herself up for decades before a friend shared, "Forgive yourself first . . . and then you will have the courage to forgive others." I have begun this practice, and it has healed me in ways, both professionally and personally, that I would have never imagined. In today's rapidly changing society, can we afford not to do this? If we, as higher education and student affairs professionals, are on the front line of providing opportunities for postsecondary education for the college-going public, we have the ability to impact these individuals during their brief time with us. Why not take advantage of this time by modeling, espousing, and acting with love and care in our work? In Chapter 6, "Dialogue, Reflection, and Learning: From Our (Spiritual) Center," Richanne Mankey notes, "Averting fear and working with ourselves and students from where we are to promote the best versions of ourselves and others is ultimately an act of unconditional love. Unconditional love is giving love to another—regardless of his or her behavior—just because the person exists. It is analogous to meeting others with positive human regard. Unconditional love promotes meeting each other at the heart level and not at the level of our own expectation or from outlined policies of behavior" (p. 96). Richanne suggests that we ask the following questions as purported by Cook (2009) to help ourselves meet each other at the heart level: In what ways might I look at the situation differently? How do I want to feel and conduct myself in this situation? In what ways might I choose to respond, not react? Meeting at the heart level allows us to use an ethic of care and love as a pathway to keep our professional practice on track.

Claim Responsibility: Professional Development Through Social Agency

We have reached a time when we must incorporate both the notions of justice and an ethic of care into our work as higher education and student affairs professionals. The corporatization of American schools of higher education is pushing us farther and farther away from the original reasons for educating individuals. It is the responsibility of a college or university to provide learning opportunities for students that help move them toward moral maturity, whereby they are caring citizens who become social agents of their villages, towns, cities, and our global community.

Calls for accountability have forced many opportunities for learning by the wayside, because we have to answer to stakeholders and other organizations that are putting statistical success above thick, rich conversations that can lead to thick, rich dialogues. Such dialogues can afford their participants opportunities to genuinely reflect *on*, and then reflect *in* action concerning situations and individuals who matter the most to them. This refocusing on the care of individuals will most likely promote communities of practice that put humans first.

We have moved beyond a time of social justice movements, where large groups of individuals mobilize to bring about social change. Rather, we now have an opportunity to empower individual learners. To help build their confidence in asking difficult questions and reflecting in action, and publicly, when appropriate, to seek understanding of a situation that may be complex and messy in nature. Building collaborative, shared communities of practice among professors and higher education and student affairs professionals could be a way to foster the integrative pedagogies supporting social agency.

Conclusion

As I reflect on my practice and attempt to hone the craft of reflecting *in* my practice, I hear the same three sentences over and over again in my mind: "Why are you doing this? What is the benefit? Is there still joy?" And so I have been trying to answer these questions. In reflecting back on my actions and also on my daily practice of reflecting in action, I knew that I did not have the answers—and I would just have to wait. Today, I am able to answer these questions, and I hope that some of what I have experienced in my professional life thus far resonates with you in your journey.

Why am I doing this? I am doing this for the same reasons that I entered the higher education and student-affairs profession. Mentors and change agents helped me along my journey, and I still believe I can impact today's college-going public in some small way, one student at a time. *What is the benefit?* If I remain student-centered, the picture is clear. Once I stop the practice of reflection, however, for the same reasons that I stop running, going to yoga, and so on, there is not as much benefit. For example, although I treasure my professional colleagues, I would still rather spend time communicating with my colleagues and students in person or via social media than "being chained to my e-mail," in the words of my new spiritual advisor, social media expert Eric Stoller. With the ability to speak "in person," using social media, comes greater responsibility than ever before to take care in communicating with individuals whom we are different from. If we start from a place of care, we can build a capacity for communicating that is dynamic in nature and is able to adapt to these rapidly changing times.

And the last question—*Is there still joy?* I am happy to report that this question was recently answered for me, in two situations. The first was when I team-taught a class in research methods at the National University of Kyiv-Mohyla Academy. Each student in class is fluent in three languages: Ukrainian, Russian, and English. We engaged in English as we discussed the Statistical Package for the Social Sciences (SPSS). Then, a student group was ready to present their overview of focus groups as a research method, and they kindly offered to present in English. When I insisted that they present in Ukrainian, they said, "But it will be in Ukrainian . . . ," and I said, "Yes— it will help me practice by listening in your language." Although they were pleased with my willingness to learn from them, I could not help but notice a small cocking of their heads. You see, they do not think in one language. And when you ask an average master's-level student in Ukraine to name the languages they know, most name three or four that they speak fluently, and then two more that they apologize for *only* being able to read or understand. If we were to approach ways in which we communicate with those we are different from as professionals, in the same ways that Ukrainian graduate students approach language acquisition, we could make some colossal advances when it comes to taking responsibility for being able to communicate with many different types of people.

The second way my question was answered was when I clicked on an e-mail from a group of amazing students from my home institution, 4,730 miles away, who sent me a YouTube video of their final presentation of focus group research projects. Seeing them and hearing their voices brought me more joy than I can ever remember experiencing! I was a bit surprised with the emotions that I was feeling, but it was at that moment that I had clarity! If I remain student-centered in my work, I will be just fine. It does not matter so much where I am at physically, because if we as humans invest the time in getting to know other humans, the mode of communication will not matter so much. And, the more that I can own my shortcomings and try to improve my relationships with others by stretching and growing, the more I can add value to another's world. Ruthie, Emily, Kia, and Latia thought nothing of the thousands of miles that separated us. They are nimble, smoothly moving between modes of communication-based technology. Their goal was to connect with me, and it did not matter to them how we connected, as long as it was personable. I am grateful to my students and hipster colleagues who encouraged me to enter the world of Facebook, then LinkedIn, Twitter, and now WordPress. Though it was a slow process for me to adapt to these new modes of technology, working through this process has helped me to recommit to the profession and reexamine how I treat others within our profession.

References

ACPA and NASPA. (2010). *Professional competency areas for student affairs practitioners.* Retreived from http://www.naspa.org/regions/regioniii/Professional%20Competency.pdf

Argyris, C., & Schön, D. A. (1974). *Theory in practice: Increasing professional effectiveness.* San Francisco, CA: Jossey-Bass.

Blundell, D. C. (2013). *8th grade paper: Comparing and contrasting the development of the printing press and the Internet.* Unpublished paper, Kyiv International School, Kyiv UA.

Bourdieu, P., & Passeron, J. C. (1990). *Reproduction in education, society and culture.* Volume 4 of Theory, culture and society. New York: Sage.

Coleman, R. M. (2012, November). *Inequality in access to higher education: A review of the literature.* Class paper presented at Buffalo State College, Buffalo, NY.

Collins, J. (2001). Good to great: *Why some companies make the leap . . . and others don't.* New York: HarperCollins.

Cook, S. G. (2009, June). Reflection: A key tool for effective leadership. *Women in Higher Education, 18*(6), 1–2.

Habermas, J. (1990). *Moral consciousness and communicative action.* Cambridge, MA: MIT Press.

Lane. J. E. (2011, Summer). Globalization of higher education: New players, new approaches. *ACPA Developments, 9*(2). Retrieved from http://www2.myacpa.org/developments/summer-2011

Odden, M. (2012, November). Good to Great *book review.* Presented at Buffalo State College, Buffalo, NY.

Pasque, P. A. (2010). *American higher education, leadership, and policy: Critical issues and the public good.* New York: Palgrave Macmillan.

Rawls, J. (2001). *Justice as fairness: A restatement.* Cambridge, MA: Belknap Press.

Stebleton, M. J., & Aleixo, M. B. (2011). Reflecting on the past: Shaping the future of student affairs. *CSPA-NYS Journal of Student Affairs, 11*(2). College Student Personnel Administrators—New York State. Retrieved from http://journals.canisius.edu/index.php/CSPANY/article/view/183/257

St. John, E. P. (2009a). *Action, reflection and social justice: Integrating moral reasoning into professional education.* Cresskill, NJ: Hampton Press.

St. John, E. P. (2009b). *College organization and professional development: Integrating moral reasoning and reflective practice.* New York: Routledge-Taylor.

CHAPTER REFLECTION QUESTIONS

Chapter 1: Seizing Responsibility (Edward P. St. John)

This chapter introduced an integrated framework for using action inquiry and reflection in pursuit of social justice in educational and administrative practice. Some reflection questions that might help readers get started in the action inquiry process follow.

1. Based on your experience as a student and professional, what social responsibilities of citizenship inform your educational and personal aspirations?
2. How do the moral and ethical codes of your profession and/or field of study inform your goals and aspirations?
3. What opportunities do you see for promoting care and justice as a student and educator?
4. Do you talk with a personal advisor, coach, or mentor about critical issues you observe?
5. What recurrent problems related to social inequality do you see in your work?
6. How might you engage colleagues in conversations about the problem, to build a shared understanding of how it came about?
7. What type of information would you need about potential causes of the problem before jumping to possible solutions?
8. What are the barriers to change within your organization—the rules, regulations, and practices—that can help solve the problem? What practices contribute to its recurrence?

Chapter 2: Actionable Knowledge and Student Affairs (Megan Moore Gardner)

1. What strategies can you employ to develop a model of professional praxis in your daily work?
2. What obstacles do you anticipate facing as you develop you professional praxis and reflect on the theories that guide your work?

3. What tools can you use to overcome those obstacles?

4. How might you already be using action research to inform your work?

5. How might you enhance and improve the use of action research to inform your work?

Chapter 3: Evolution of a Moral and Caring Professional (Kathleen M. Boyle)

1. When thinking about personal and professional action, what role does consciousness play?

2. What are the connections among care, justice, an ethic of care, and social justice?

3. How does one act deliberately? How does this differ from acting?

4. How will you challenge yourself to reflect and ponder "vexing problems"—looking for multiple perspectives to construct a meaningful argument or proposal that acknowledges the uncertainty of knowledge? Who will support you in being a reflective practitioner? How will you seek their assistance?

5. Ask yourself: Who am I? Have you reflected on your own psychosocial, identity, cognitive, and moral development? How does this have an impact on those you come in contact with?

6. How have you challenged yourself to understand those who hold different identities from your own?

7. What aspects of working with others different from you do you find challenging? How do you work within and through these challenges?

8. How will you intentionally create spaces for open dialogue and developmental conversations within your work (not merely "chatting" with others, but striving for intentionally meaningful conversations that present opportunities to be contemplatives in action)?

9. How can anyone be a deliberate actor or a contemplative in action when she or he finds herself or himself "putting out fires" and reacting to the real or perceived immediate needs of various groups (students, supervisors, parents, administrators, etc.)?

10. What do you know, and what do you need to learn, about other cultures? How do you open up space, express value, and integrate others into your work and life?

Chapter 4: Critical Social Dialogues and Reflecting in Action (Shakira Henderson and Kimberly A. Kline)

1. What are some ways to effectively build rapport among professors and students?
2. How can we identify self-censorship in the classroom?
3. What are some ways we can discourage self-censorship both within the role of student and practitioner?
4. Name ways in which student affairs practitioners can encourage students to move beyond compassion toward more meaningful social justice orientation?
5. Can you think of a past course that you have taken that has omitted themes of social justice? How would you have integrated social justice into the course? What would've been the limitations?
6. What are some examples of "insincere politically correct language"?
7. Have you ever witnessed "insincere politically correct language" being used? What was its effect on the dialogue?
8. Have you ever participated in a social justice oriented course? If so how did your participation influence your approach to other classes or unrelated situations?

Chapter 5: The Game Changers (Wanda M. Davis)

1. What can campuses do to assess campus climate?
2. What role does student affairs play in creating a civil learning environment on campus?
3. What personal responsibility do you have in addressing uncivil behavior on campus?
4. Identify three major issues that will affect campus climate over the next 3–5 years.
5. What strategies can you identify to address these issues?
6. How can technology help in addressing campus climate issues?

Chapter 6: Dialogue, Reflection, and Learning (Richanne C. Mankey)

1. If any of the "tools" in this chapter resonate with you, how might you use them to further facilitate your journey of self-understanding to benefit you professionally and personally?

2. In what ways might I take appropriate "risks" that promote student learning and build positive communities?
3. In what ways might I incorporate more listening into my daily inter-actions?
4. In what ways might I better develop my own reflective practice?
5. In what ways might I more consistently practice the beliefs and values I treasure?
6. In what ways might I become increasingly more aware of any role that FEAR plays in my life and profession?
7. From the narrative, in situations I face as a professional and a person:
   a. In what ways might I look at situations differently?
   b. How do I want to feel and conduct myself in these situations?
   c. In what ways might I evaluate if I am responding or reacting? (Cook, 2009)
   d. In what ways am I promoting transformative learning in myself and others?
8. From the narrative and related to the five agreements:
   a. In what ways have I used my words impeccably?
   b. In what ways have I made any assumptions?
   c. In what ways have I taken something someone said or did personally?
   d. In what ways have I given my best?
   e. In what ways have I listened with compassion for the person and skepticism of myself?
9. Am I playing the finite or the infinite game? (Carse, 1986)
10. In what ways are my actions and words contributing to students becoming the most effective and aware graduates they can be?

Chapter 7: Reflection in Action (Pamela Petrease Felder)

One method for addressing racial and cultural issues as teaching priorities is to reflect on these issues in a teaching narrative. This reflective narrative can be developed in as little as 10–15 minutes (or longer depending on the depth and nature of your reflection) by focusing on the following questions:

1. Why is teaching about race and culture important to you?
2. How do you know this? How can you confirm this level of impor-tance by way of your behavior (inside/outside of the classroom)?
3. In what ways are race and culture part of your teaching priorities?
4. Are these priorities addressed on a consistent basis? If so, in what way?

5. In what ways do these priorities align (or not align) with research literature focused on teaching race and culture? Please consider your discipline.

Chapter 8: Teaching Professional Development in Higher Education and Student Affairs (Stacy A. Jacob)

1. Take a moment to think about the larger professional goals you have had for yourself in the past. These goals can include your professional aspirations as a child, subsequent professional aspirations, how you chose your college major, various professional and educational goals you have for yourself, and any professional development opportunities in which you have participated. Reflect and write about important life points related to your various professional goals, making sure to detail your thoughts as best you can. What themes in all of these writings can you find? How does examining the prevalent themes in your life help guide your future professional development?

2. Read or watch the movie version of *The Lorax*. Identify the "trees"— the things you are most passionate about advocating for—in your professional life. Explain why these trees are important to you. What further training do you need to be a better advocate for these trees? Research the types of training that you could complete and develop a professional development plan so that you may better serve these trees.

3. Think about the various parts of you and jot down which areas you believe you may need to develop further. Identify these areas and explain why you think they need attention. Outline ways in which you may develop these parts of you and construct a plan to explore and develop them.

4. Identify a list of professionals whom you respect and whose work, opinions, attitudes, or ideas you value. Create a set of interview questions to help you uncover important advice from these professionals, then plan and conduct interviews with them.

Chapter 9: Moving From Social Justice to Social Agency (Penny A. Pasque and Brittany Harris)

1. What oppressive and discriminatory acts on college campuses are conscious and easy to see? What acts may be currently unconscious, difficult to identify, or identified and articulated by our peers?

2. Recognizing social injustice versus acting on that injustice are two different, albeit related, things. In what ways have you acted as an advocate, ally, and/or agent of change that upset the status quo in front of and behind closed doors?

3. Describe any specific incidents that have happened on your campus that connect issues of oppression across race, ethnicity, class, gender, sexual orientation, religion, ability, age, nationality, size, and additional social identities and the intersections of these identities. In what ways do issues of power, privilege, oppression, violence, perceptions of masculinity, fear, crisis, public shame, intimidation, threats, residence life, Greek Life, athletics, classrooms, technology, alcohol, and/or myriad other issues show up in these incidents? What can you do on campus to react to these situations? What can do you do to be proactive?

4. How do the three *D*s (dialogue, disregard, and dissonance) show up in your life? How do notions of (in)civility show up on your campus?

5. Have you developed a "mask of survival," or masked your inner self to not show inner feelings, as a way to defend against oppression or discrimination in educational institutions and/or as a means of self-protection? In what ways does this help and hurt you or other people on campus with your same (different) social identities?

6. How can you stay "checked-in" and engage in the dialogue or step out, process with a peer, counselor, and/or facilitator, and then re-engage next time the group is together? How can you push on your own learning edges in ways that may help you or your group to understand issues of social justice in a different way and figure out what this means as you move toward social agency? In what ways might you develop a "healthy resistance"?

7. Becoming a community of practice is an ongoing process that takes open dialogue, patience, and a willingness to unpack your "stuff" (e.g., identities, past experiences). What tools, trainings, or strategies have you created to ensure that you are fostering a safe, inclusive community for not only your students, but for your peers as well?

ABOUT THE EDITOR AND CONTRIBUTORS

Editor

Kimberly A. Kline serves as associate professor of higher education administration at Buffalo State, State University of New York. Her research focuses on professional development, issues of social justice/agency in higher education, and student learning outcomes assessment. She had the privilege of serving as a 2012–2013 Fulbright Scholar at the National University of Kyiv-Mohyla Academy in Ukraine.

Kimberly is interested in helping campuses develop grassroots efforts to promote student learning and development. She earned a PhD in higher education from Indiana University, an MS in student personnel administration from Buffalo State, and a BA in political science from Slippery Rock University.

Contributors

Kathleen "Kate" M. Boyle is an associate professor in the Department of Leadership, Policy, and Administration at The University of St. Thomas (UST). She is in her tenth year as the program director for the Leadership in Student Affairs master's degree program and in the Leadership doctoral program. She graduated with her PhD in higher education administration from Indiana University and her master's degree in counseling and student personnel services from Minnesota State at Mankato. he recently coedited a monograph for ACPA–College Student Educators International entitled *Reflections on the 75th Anniversary of the Student Personnel Point of View*. Her research interests include issues of gender and women's history, professional socialization and identity development, and college student and adult development.

Wanda M. Davis is professor and chair of the Higher Education Administration Department at Buffalo State, with research interests that include the history of American higher education and the study of social movements. Davis serves on national editorial boards and has numerous publications. Serving in just about every level of management in student affairs, she also served in academic administration as assistant vice provost and associate vice president for undergraduate studies, and she obtained major grants from the New York Council of the Humanities. Davis served as a National Endowment for the Humanities (NEH) Fellow at Harvard University.

Pamela Petrease Felder is a lecturer in the Higher Education Division in the Graduate School of Education at The University of Pennsylvania. Her primary research interests involve examining inequities in doctoral degree attainment by considering the racial and cultural experiences of graduate students (with an emphasis on the doctoral experience). This includes the impact of prior socialization experiences and student perspectives of institutional climate and student–faculty relationships on academic achievement and success.

Brittany Harris is the Education and Outreach Coordinator for the Penn Women's Center at The University of Pennsylvania. She received her MEd in adult and higher education, student affairs administration, at the University of Oklahoma in 2012. A native of St. Louis, Missouri, Brittany has a BS in corporate communication with a minor in Africana studies from the University of Central Missouri. She is a social justice advocate and very passionate about improving issues concerning underrepresented students in higher education.

Shakira Henderson, raised in Brooklyn, currently calls Buffalo, New York, home. Shakira's primary research interests include how race, gender, and relationship status influence academic and cocurricular decision-making among minority female graduate students. She is also interested in classroom identities assumed by the children of US emigrants during K–12 education, and how these identities influence their paths to college readiness; attendance; and, ultimately, completion. In her free time, Shakira enjoys reading, trying new recipes, and hosting themed dinner parties.

Stacy A. Jacob is an assistant professor of student affairs in higher education at Slippery Rock University. Her administrative career spanned several functional areas in higher education including admissions, residence life, Greek life, and academic support. Stacy's main research interests are the scholarship of teaching and learning (SoTL) within the field of student affairs and higher education, college choice, and the history of student affairs and higher education. Much of her work also addresses various social justice issues. Stacy earned her PhD in Higher Education at Indiana University.

Richanne C. Mankey has served higher education since 1983 and is currently interim vice president for institutional advancement/vice president for student affairs at Daemen College. She holds degrees from Teachers College, Columbia University (doctorate); University of Dayton (master's); and Ohio Northern University (bachelor's). Mankey's interest in leadership and learning was inspired by her doctoral research and her studies of the Mayan calendar's positive implications for human consciousness evolution. Reflection and meditation have become tools for her continued holistic growth and development—she believes we are perfectly imperfect. Mankey has presented internationally and domestically on student learning, student affairs, and leadership.

Megan Moore Gardner is an associate professor of higher education administration at the University of Akron. She currently teaches courses in assessment, higher education policy and accountability, organizational behavior, leadership in student affairs/services, and student development theory. Before transitioning to faculty, Megan spent a number of years working in administrative roles in student affairs. Her research focuses on a variety of topics including curricular and cocurricular assessment, professional development and accountability in higher education, Catholic higher education, and issues of social justice in higher education.

Penny A. Pasque is an associate professor of adult and higher education in the departments of Educational Leadership and Policy Studies, Women's and Gender Studies, and the Center for Social Justice at the University of Oklahoma. She also serves as a visiting scholar with the Center for the Study of Higher and Postsecondary Education and the Center for the Education of Women at the University of Michigan for the 2013–2014 academic year. Her research addresses in/equities in higher education and student affairs, dis/connections between higher education and society, and complexities in critical qualitative inquiry.

Edward P. St. John, Algo D. Henderson Collegiate Professor of Higher Education at the University of Michigan's Center for the Study of Higher and Postsecondary Education, is concerned with education for a just society, an interest that stems from three decades of research on educational policy and practice. He is a Fellow of the American Educational Research Association and has received awards for leadership and research from the Association for the Study of Higher Education. His most recent book, *Research, Actionable Knowledge, and Social Change*, launched Stylus Publishing's Actionable Research for Social Justice in Higher Education book series in 2013.

on providing practical solutions rather than sociopolitical analysis is refreshing, and is enormously useful in addressing a vital, pressing issue."

—*Robert Shireman,*
Director, California Competes, and former U.S. Deputy
Undersecretary of Education

Sty/us

22883 Quicksilver Drive
Sterling, VA 20166-2102

Subscribe to our e-mail alerts: www.Styluspub.com

Also available from Stylus

Research, Actionable Knowledge, and Social Change
Reclaiming Social Responsibility Through Research Partnerships

**Actionable Research for Social Justice in
Education and Society series**
Edward P. St. John
Foreword by Penny A. Pasque

This is the inaugural volume in the Actionable Research for Social Justice in Education and Society series. Written for social science researchers, practitioners, and students, this professional text provides strategies and frameworks for using social science research to engage in critical social and educational problem solving. It is based on lessons learned and insights gained over four decades from the author's work in evaluating interventions, conducting policy research, and supporting university partnerships with schools and community organizations. Combining critical analysis and traditional research methods, this book offers guidance for using the action inquiry model (AIM), a transformative model for successfully conducting action-oriented research in a multitude of professional service organizations. It aims to encourage a new generation of research-based partnerships and reforms that promote equity and access for under-served populations.

This book provides researchers with a meta-methodology for using both quantitative and qualitative methods that meets peer-reviewed publication standards while working in partnership settings. It is also appropriate for students enrolled in higher education master's and doctoral programs and other programs that involve social science research, providing practical guidance for developing dissertations and other research projects that support social change, promote student justice, and contribute to the research literature. Using this text in research design courses will facilitate open discussion of the practical problems encountered in the research process.

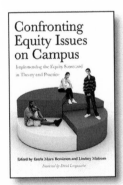

Confronting Equity Issues on Campus
Implementing the Equity Scorecard in Theory and Practice
Edited by Estela Mara Bensimon and Lindsey Malcolm
Foreword by David Longanecker

"The accountability mechanisms imposed by policy makers frequently fail to provide insight where it is most needed – in the classroom and in the other important interactions between practitioners and students. The methods detailed in Confronting Equity Issues on Campus bridge that gap, fueling the feedback loop that helps faculty and administrators test their assumptions, revise practices, and improve student outcomes. The book's focus